PRACTICAL ALGORITHMS ON LARGE DATASETS

PRACTICAL ALGORITHMS ON LARGE DATASETS

Vadim Stadnik

ISBN-13: 978-0-646-80637-2

Table of Contents

Foreword

The ease of using in programming solutions basic data structures (arrays, linked lists and balanced search trees) comes at the high cost of performance problems when the size of a user dataset becomes large. This book describes how to solve these problems using advanced data structures that are capable of supporting a wide variety of efficient primary operations required in an application domain. This ability enables us not only to address the performance issues but also to develop general purpose programming tools without loss of efficiency.

The focus is on efficient algorithms for data processing and analysis: the summation, the computation of statistical characteristics, such as the mean and the standard deviation, range queries, search and modifying operations on both ordered and unordered datasets. These algorithms play important role in applications that deal with constantly growing volumes of data. We pay special attention to the computer representation of sets, sequences and other mathematical concepts effective in numerous applications areas.

This book aims to show the significant potential of advanced data structures. To help readers gain confidence in solving real-world problems, we illustrate main ideas with introductory variants of these data structures and take advantage of the geometric interpretation. It might be surprising that some aspects of advanced data structures are not extremely challenging.

Chapter 1: Introduction

This book provides an introduction to efficient algorithms on large datasets, which are stored in advanced data structures. The common view is that this is quite a challenging domain of computer science and mathematics. By definition, advanced data structures cannot be simple. In practice, however, some of them are simpler than others. To better understand this point, consider basic data structures. Arrays and linked lists are easier for coding than trees. As the complexity of data structures increases, the situation remains the same. Programmers are more comfortable with skip lists rather than with trees that have a branching structure. This fact enables us to choose the data structures the most appropriate for an explanation of main ideas. The introductory variants in this book have a level linked structure that looks like an arrangement of lists in a skip list. They represent simplified B+-trees, which are the data structures of the main choice in applications processing large datasets.

The performance characteristics of algorithms and the design of data structures are closely tied to each other. For this reason, the book discusses basic principles and methods of designing efficient algorithms. This knowledge is important for the development of modern software systems, since the variety of specific data structures and their programming implementations is very wide and continues to grow, whereas the number of principles and methods remains relatively small. The fundamental nature of these methods will help the reader to develop new efficient algorithms not only in the introductory but also in other types of data structures described in textbooks and articles. In this context, the specific algorithms and data structures in this book can be viewed as illustrations for the design methods.

The improved performance of a desired algorithm can be achieved by modifying properties of a given data structure. One of the main design methods discussed in this book is the method of augmenting a data structure. A modified data structure is named an augmented data structure. To distinguish it from a basic data structure, such as an array, a linked list or a search tree, we also use the name advanced data structure.

The attractive feature of this method is the ease of developing new algorithms and, thus, extending the set of efficient operations required in a user algorithm. The running time of an operation is usually reduced from linear to logarithmic. An increase in the number of primary operations with such a performance improvement has the effect of converting ordinary computing devices into supercomputers. The important practical advantage of such performance improvements is that they can be implemented in most computer systems.

In simple applications, the design methods allow us to address performance issues caused by brute force algorithms. For large and complex software systems, the benefits of using these methods are substantially greater. The most effective programming solutions are based on the fundamental mathematical concepts, such as a set and a sequence. The properly modified data structures offer the enhanced facilities for the computer representation of fundamental mathematical concepts. Because of a high level of generality, these representations can be used in a wide variety of applications. Unlike basic data structures, the generality of the representations based on advanced data structures does not exclude the efficiency.

1.1 PREREQUISITES

This book is written for anyone who would like to extend knowledge of efficient algorithms for large datasets that can be used in many practical applications. This objective assumes that the reader is prepared for the content of this book.

The minimum is knowledge of basic data structures: arrays, linked lists, binary trees, B- and B+-trees and skip lists. A good understanding of linked structures of nodes is quite important, because arrays are not always the best choice for explaining key ideas. It would be also helpful to be familiar with the basics of graph theory and the method of augmenting data structures.

One chapter of this book provides an overview of basic data structures and algorithms. However, the scope of this chapter is reduced to topics important in the context of this book. For an in-depth coverage, the reader should refer to excellent books on classical algorithms and data structures.

The choice of the appropriate terminology for the introductory description of algorithms on advanced data structures is both important and non-trivial. It has been one of the most challenging aspects of the work on this book. The decision has been made to provide a relatively simple (but not oversimplified) explanation. This approach has been suggested by practical lessons, which showed that, these days, many developers and programmers are not comfortable with formal and highly abstract mathematical concepts, such as "topological space", "metric space", "strict weak ordering", "partially ordered set" and so on. Such knowledge is certainly helpful for reading this book, but not required. We prefer simpler concepts, such as "distance" and "comparison". In addition, for the illustration of key ideas we use the geometric interpretation.

1.2 MOTIVATION

This book reflects the experience gained from the development of various advanced data structures and efficient algorithms. The shape and value of this software are significantly affected by the differences in the needs of specific applications and in the mathematical background of programmers (both novices and experts).

One of the main design issues of many implementations is that the big potential of advanced data structures is used to offer solutions to narrow application domains. Such variants do not take advantage of a wide set of efficient operations that these data structures support. The important aspect of the generalization is often underestimated and ignored.

The other issues are associated with the internal complexity of advanced data structures. The benefits of these data structures come at the high cost of development. Because such data structures are not always available in standard libraries, programmers develop their own extensions. And it is not unusual that a developer who worked on a project may not easily understand and be able to maintain the code written by another developer. Even when the code quality is high, the other programmer remains concerned about potential issues of the complex code and is reluctant to use such non-standard extensions in his or her solutions. Except for the author, programmers cannot take full advantage of the custom implementation.

The lessons learnt from this practical experience helped us to identify a number of common misunderstandings in the development of advanced data structures. The main source of confusion with both developers and users is the computer representation of a mathematical sequence. Arrays and linked lists are traditionally viewed as the best and even only choice for algorithms using sequences. Trees are normally overlooked, since many do not believe that a properly designed tree can replace these basic data structures and deliver significant performance improvements.

There is also some confusion about implementation approaches and application domains for B-trees and B+-trees. This should be less surprising, since these trees were originally designed for databases stored in external memory and descriptions of on-disk variants of these trees are the most common in textbooks.

The main objective of textbooks is to provide an explanation of basic data structures and simplest variants of algorithms. The textbook examples may not work well in practice. For example, efficient algorithms based on recursive function calls are avoided in solutions for large scale problems.

The description of advanced data structures is insufficient for a wide use, because they are considered as extensions of basic data structures for specific applications. In particular, the order statistics trees are explained in a number of books, but the fact that the same data structures can be used as efficient sequences is not normally discussed.

At the same time, the advanced data structures are one of the most dynamic areas of fundamental research in computer science. One might expect that the high activity in this research area helps programmers easily create new innovative products and improve customer satisfaction. This is true to some degree only. The research articles and books are written at the highest level of abstraction in mathematics and computer science. This literature is not an easy reading for practitioners. When it comes to the practical development, programmers face many challenges of understanding theoretical results obtained by researchers and writing code in a specific programming language for a specific system. It is hard to find in research literature the best answers to numerous implementation specific questions. This situation, however, should not disappoint those programmers and software engineers who enjoy closing the gap between theoretical findings and successful software products.

This book addresses some of the issues mentioned earlier. However, the discussion of typical misunderstandings is not the main goal of this book. The advanced data structures have significant potential for solving a wide variety of problems, which is why it is important to know how to take full advantage of this power in practice. We would like to help the reader to gain confidence in the use of this power.

1.3 METHODS FOR ACHIEVING HIGH PERFORMANCE

The performance is one of the key measures of the value of a computer system and/or a software product. Its importance in practical applications can be hardly overestimated. The high performance is not only a competitive advantage. It is also a factor that determines success of a product or a business. The most advanced computer systems have the ability to store the largest datasets and process huge number of transactions in the minimum amount of time. These systems have reached the computational power to provide global services for billions of users. However, the need for high performance arises in small to medium scale applications too, because it is economically profitable for users. In business, the pressure of delivering desired results is enormous. Poor performance of a program leads to unacceptable delays and a high cost of a product or a service. It affects customers' satisfaction, in which case they switch to another program or system. The high performance in the form of real time processing is a "must have" requirement for many modern applications of computers. It is also a sign of a high quality. The benefits of efficient programs and services are the driving force for the investment into performance improvements of software products and computer systems.

Achieving the high performance faces numerous technological and theoretical challenges. The specific factors, which define the progress, vary from system to system. In the general case, the two main methods of achieving high performance follow from the obvious fact that a program is executed on a computer system.

The first method is to increase computing power by upgrading hardware. The strength of this method is that it is supported by the continuous increase in the number of processors, CPU speed and memory capacity of a single computer system. The technological advances make the hardware computing power more affordable, but this is not a cheap method to deliver desired results.

The issue of matching hardware cost against problem size and complexity is a fundamental limitation of this method in practice. An increase in the number of processors in combination with the straightforward parallelization of computations offers only linear growth in computing power of a system. The hardware improvement using such an algorithmic method is ineffective to address the issues of exponential growth in data volumes. These challenges require different approaches to take advantage of the hardware power.

The second method of achieving high performance and addressing performance issues is the optimization of software for the application needs. The focus of this book is on the algorithmic variant of this method that delivers a significant performance improvement, typically from linear to logarithmic. To illustrate its idea, compare the performance of search operations on two data structures of linked nodes: a list and a balanced tree. A linked list does not support the running time better than linear. This data structure should be avoided in applications that frequently search data. A balanced tree is a much better choice, since it offers operations that take logarithmic time.

The key advantage of the optimization method is the substantially smaller number of operations executed. It is much more cost effective against equivalent hardware upgrades, since it delivers a desired result without buying expensive hardware. Alternatively, using hardware upgrade to achieve the running time of an optimal algorithm may not be practical because of prohibitive cost of hardware.

1.4 INEFFICIENCIES IN SOFTWARE PRODUCTS

The most typical performance problems in software products are caused by basic data structures and brute force algorithms, first of all, because they are heavily used in standard libraries. In addition to this, not every software product needs the best algorithms. The performance of a commercial product must simply meet customer's requirements. The high quality of software has a high cost of development and maintenance. Product deliver deadline is a big factor in the real-world development. Even experienced programmers use brute force algorithms and basic data structures, since they offer the advantage of the minimal cost of development. Simple but not the most efficient algorithms are acceptable at this stage.

The situation may change in the future, when the hidden problems become real. This is the case when a customer wants to process large datasets on a new more powerful computer system that offers a significant increase in the size of main memory and only a small improvement of CPU speed. The request is easy to implement in software products based on standard containers, which are designed to run on various systems. For well-designed software products, the hardware upgrade improves the overall performance. But sometime a product on a better platform becomes surprisingly less responsive.

Unfortunately, the portability of the code and the significant increase in the capacity of fast internal memory do not always guarantee desired results in terms of performance. A product is originally developed and tested for a problem size and a computer system specified by a user. The basic data structures in standard containers work fine on any compatible computer system. Switching to a new more powerful system enables a user to process larger datasets. As the size of a user dataset increases, the inefficient operations on the basic data structures sharply increase their contribution to the total running time. In sequential processing, the common cause of the performance degradation is a primary operation that takes linear time. For example, an iterative method, which searches for positions and inserts new elements into an array, has quadratic performance. This is a typical performance issue when originally chosen data structures and algorithms have not been designed for a bigger problem size.

One of the practical methods to deal with performance problems in software products is the development of a new solution using an improved business model. The task requires thorough analysis of all of the supporting operations and their frequencies in a given use case. In a relatively rare best-case scenario, the new solution has a similar structure but is based on different data structures that provide improved efficiency of the most frequent operations. The method of application specific improvements is normally acceptable, but it has a high cost of development and misses the opportunity to make software more general and re-usable.

1.5 OPTIMIZATION OF DATA STRUCTURES

This book concentrates on the method of choosing or developing the optimal data structure, which provides efficient primary operations required in client code. This method is general and cost effective in the most complex software products, since it supports a simple drop-in replacement for inefficient data structures and operations. In the example of sequential processing using an array, the overall performance can be substantially improved if the array is replaced by a balanced tree, which provides both search and insertion operations that take logarithmic time.

The practical implementation of this method assumes that an appropriate data structure is available in a software product or a general purpose library. Quite obviously, this is not always the case. And the cost of not having right components in such a library can become quite significant, because as a project evolves the code becomes more complicated due to unavoidable dependencies between the library and new clients. This is one of the reasons why it is important to know how to develop new efficient data structures or improve performance of existing data structures.

This book discusses the design of efficient data structures that effectively addresses the typical issues of poor performance in software products. In many specific cases, we solve these problems by adding new efficient algorithms on user datasets. With a small amount of effort, we implement the incremental algorithmic improvements that extend the set of efficient primary operation supported by a data structure. This approach provides important benefits, which we discuss below.

Any basic data structure, such as a list or an array, is capable of providing a wide variety of operations for user algorithms. However, the running time of primary operations on these data structures differs quite significantly: from constant to linear. Complex algorithms that require different types of operations on a dataset are often based on several basic data structures. The performance is optimized by using the most efficient operations of each data structure involved. This approach has a potential performance problem that inefficient operations may have quite significant effect on the overall computational cost.

The important advantage of a solution using one advanced data structure over a solution using several basic data structures is that a properly designed advanced data structure does not have any inefficient operation that can cause a performance problem. For programming solutions, the wide set of efficient operations supported by one data structure opens great opportunity to achieve a high level of generality without loss of efficiency.

Unlike application specific solutions that can be developed in cooperation with business experts only, the design of data structures and algorithms for general purposes does not make any assumptions about frequencies of specific operations involved. Ideally, each operation must be as efficient as possible. A more practical requirement is to minimize the number of inefficient operations that take linear time. However, this approach risks performance issues similar to those caused by basic data structures and brute force algorithms.

The methods described in this book enable us to reduce the running time of primary operations from linear to logarithmic. When we use B+ trees with a small number of levels, the running time achieved is basically constant. This performance improvement is adequate for general purpose facilities to replace basic data structures in complex solutions. Compared to the application specific approach, the general purpose facilities guarantee a significantly lower cost of development of new programming solutions in a broad range of applications. This benefit is super linear with the increase in the problem complexity.

1.6 APPLICATIONS

In this book, our interest is in the processing of large and possibly huge volumes of data. The high performance algorithms are of critical importance in these applications. The balanced search trees support various efficient searches, range queries, insertions and deletions. However, they are not normally optimized for data analysis, problem solving and modeling that involve the computation of the key statistical parameters, such as the mean and the standard deviation. The addition of such high-performance facilities would be very beneficial for practical applications. The advanced data structures and algorithms described in this book offer the facilities, which supersede the facilities of arrays, linked lists, and search trees. Their important advantage over search trees is that they efficiently process both ordered and unordered datasets.

At the level of primary operations, the functionality required for data analysis is based on the addition and summation. We use the method of augmenting a data structure for the design of new efficient algorithms. This method enables us to add the required facilities by implementing the fast summation algorithm as a primary operation.

The modified data structure guarantees logarithmic running time of the summation and the computation of main statistical parameters. This is a significant improvement compared to the standard sequential summation that has linear running time. The improvement cannot be achieved with basic data structures, such as arrays or linked lists. These fast sequential summation algorithms are superior to the parallel summation algorithms. It is also not too difficult to implement the new efficient algorithms, which find minimum and maximum values in any range of consecutive elements. This is another important extension required in processing of large datasets. All of these additional operations are as efficient as a search for a single key in a balanced search tree.

The fast summation algorithms are the focus of this book because of their fundamental theoretical and practical importance. Unlike basic search algorithms, the fast sequential summation algorithms use both addition and search operations. This is an interesting feature for historical reasons. The very first application of computers was solving numerical problems. The substantial increase in storage space along with the invention of efficient sorting and searching has made computers irreplaceable tools in solving non-numerical problems - the application area, which is broadly named information processing. The efficient summation algorithms involve basic operations specific to both of these application areas.

In many practical applications, the best performance is achieved with array-based algorithms. At the same time, these variants of fast summation algorithms are challenging for understanding. In this context, the data structure and algorithms proposed by Fenwick are particularly mysterious. To help the reader, we introduce for an explanation a matching linked data structure, which addresses the issues of the implicit array representation.

1.7 PROGRAMMING LANGUAGES AND CODE

Many algorithms discussed in this book have been originally developed and tested in C++. This language offers a wide variety of facilities that allow programmers to write efficient and portable code with the optimal cost of development and maintenance. It has proven to be effective in solutions to numerous practical problems. In the context of this book, the strength of C++ is in its ability to support mathematical concepts, models and solutions to challenging problems.

The downside of this language is its complexity. The introductory description of efficient algorithms aims to minimize the impact of programming technicalities, which become quite numerous when we write real code. The language and system details are important at the stage of developing and fine-tuning specialized algorithms that deliver the best possible performance. Such optimization methods are beyond the scope of this book. This approach allows us to focus on main ideas, design methods and essential properties of data structures with the goal of developing efficient algorithms on user datasets.

Another important advantage of ignoring implementation specific technicalities is that it helps us to find variants of algorithms and data structures, which form the basis of general purpose libraries. Such variants provide elegant interfaces for various application areas and protect users from the implementation complexity.

The ideas and design methods discussed in this book can be used to develop algorithms and data structures in many programming languages, such as C, C++, C# and Java. The basic variants require that a language provides arrays and pointers or references that avoid copying large datasets and objects. A developer does not have to be skilled in programming techniques to implement these entry-level variants. With experience, however, comes the understanding of the benefits of code reuse through abstraction. The support for object-oriented programming and generic programming based on templates would significantly ease the practical development of advanced general purpose variants of algorithms and data structures.

The code in this book has been written for illustration purposes only. We use only a small subset of basic C++ features in order to simplify its translation to other programming languages. It is not supposed to be directly used in a software product. The real code deals with many non-trivial issues. At the low level of abstraction and modeling these are numerical errors, division by zero, overflow and underflow errors. In addition, high-quality commercial and open source implementations are portable. The main challenge of the top level of abstraction is the representation of fundamental mathematical concepts, such as a set and a sequence. The appropriate implementation would benefit from the generic programming technique. These programming aspects are beyond the scope of this book.

1.8 MODEL OF COMPUTATION

This book is intended for practical applications. The analysis of algorithms is not rigorous, since theoretical computational complexities are not always correct in practice. We use a random access machine (RAM) model of computation. A computer system represents a single processor with the main memory large enough to store a given dataset or a data structure. To avoid complicating factors we normally ignore the internal complexity of the memory hierarchy in real systems: several levels of processor cache and external storage.

The idealized computer system provides constant time access to any data element stored in an array. For a linked data structure, the system guarantees constant time of traversing a link between any two adjacent nodes. A distant node is reached in linear time in the number of links connecting two given nodes. An algorithm is a sequence of operations executed one at a time. No concurrent operations on a data structures are allowed. The performance of an algorithm does not depend on the size of a dataset.

Despite a bit unrealistic assumptions, this simple abstract model is useful in the initial analysis and design of algorithms. It is suitable for the first order approximation and asymptotical estimates. The performance-critical algorithms and sections of code are optimized using measurements on specific computer systems.

Chapter 2: Overview of Basic Data Structures

Each data structure provides a number of efficient operations that help us develop the optimal solution for one type of user problems. However, in a solution to another type of user problems this data structure can be outperformed by other data structures. The lack of a single data structure perfect for numerous practical applications explains the reason why well-designed software libraries offer a variety of data structures with different performance characteristics.

This chapter compares the running time of primary operations on several fundamental data structures in the context of processing of large datasets. The comparison is important to identify limitations and inefficient operations that can cause performance degradation of a user algorithm. In the following chapters, we will address the performance issues by developing improved variants of data structures that support faster operations for user algorithms.

The performance of all of the operations supported by a data structure depends on two main design choices:

- a structure, which represents a connectivity of nodes in a linked data structure or cells in an array;
- a data scheme, which specifies how data elements are organized and stored in nodes or cells of this data structure.

It is important to note that one structure of connected nodes or cells can be used with more than one data scheme. This fact simplifies the analysis and design of data structures. It also allows us to consider these two aspects of the design of algorithms separately.

Solving a challenging problem is not a straightforward matter. The design of a high performance data structure is very challenging. Finding a solution to this type of problems is an iterative process, which involves several cycles of improvements to the selected structure and the data scheme. The topology of a cycle does not prioritize elements involved. There is no least or most significant element. It is the developer responsibility to choose the first element in the cycle to start the development. What do we start with: the structure or the data scheme?

In our opinion, it is more reasonable to start the analysis with the structure than with the data scheme, since the connectivity of nodes determines the performance of such important operations as the insertion, deletion and search. The common feature of high performance data structures is that they grow and contract in the same way regardless of specific data, which they store. A data structure is shaped by the balance rules and its specific invariants. A data scheme controls the position of inserting or deleting an element, but it has no effect on structural invariants. On the other hand, modifying operations on a data structure are responsible for maintaining not only structural but also data scheme invariants. We can simplify the initial analysis and design by avoiding the complications associated with details of a data scheme. The subsequent iterations will improve the design.

At early stages of a design, it is useful to consider a data structure as a structured storage, which provides the space to store user data elements in nodes, if it is a linked data structure, or in cells, if it is an array. The data structure plays a role of a mediator between a system and a user algorithm. For example, the link-based data structures are usually dynamically allocated, which is why they are space efficient. In basic data structures, nodes or cells store objects of a fixed size. When a node is created, a memory region for a data element either stores its default value or remains uninitialized. Specific keys and values are not required at this stage.

The efficiency of access to elements stored in a data structure_is very important for the overall performance of user algorithms. Slow access is unacceptable for the high performance solutions. The best data structures provide constant time access to an arbitrary element. Less efficient data structures, such as linked lists, provide fast access only to the nearest neighbours of a given element. This performance is acceptable for sequential processing of data.

Access operations are relatively simple compared to other types of operations. They are implemented through search algorithms that do not modify a data structure. The algorithms differ in details and have different performance properties. This is why, it is desirable to estimate the best possible performance of access operations on a selected data structure. This can be done using the connectivity of nodes and the length of the shortest path between two distant nodes of the data structure. This performance may not be attainable due to restrictions of a data scheme. However, such estimates are useful to discard data structures with inefficient access at early stages of the analysis and design.

Despite some limitations, basic data structures are a good choice for a wide variety of applications. They are good examples of the general purpose tools, which are simple and effective. For specific applications, the connectivity of nodes in a data structure can be fine-tuned to optimize the performance of required operations. However, this improvement may come at the expense of higher complexity and increased running time of other primary operations. Finding the optimal structure that supports high performance of a wide set of primary operations is the area of the design of advanced data structures.

We begin with the basic linked data structures, which are easier to understand than implicit array representations.

2.1 PROPERTIES OF LINKED DATA STRUCTURES

2.1.1 Linear Data Structures

The linked lists are the simplest data structures of linked nodes. They are linear and one-dimensional in terms of a method that connects two nodes in a list. Similar to a line segment, a linear structure of a list has two ends. In order to deal with the irregularity of boundary conditions, programming implementations of linked lists often use special end nodes, such as head and tail. The other implementation approach is based on a circular list. It is more convenient in many practical cases, since it requires one special node instead of two. A circular list that has only such a special node represents an empty dataset.

In a singly linked list, each node knows a next node only (see Figure 2.1). This data structure is designed for efficient one way traversal. Access to a previous node is possible because of the implementation choice. It is slow and should be avoided in practice.

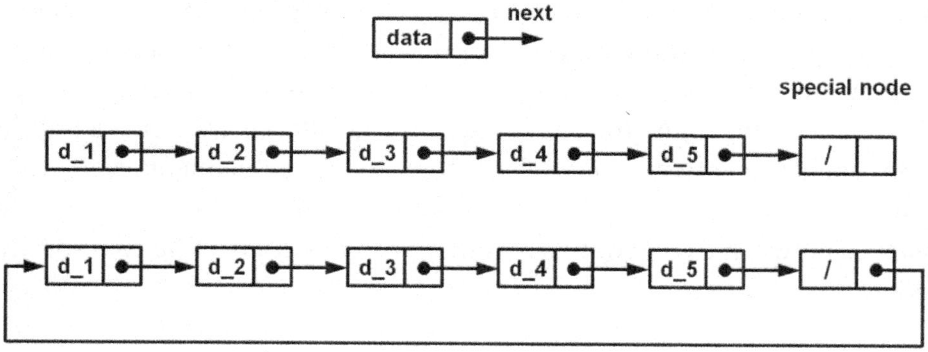

Figure 2.1: A singly linked list that stores 5 data elements and its representation using a circular list.

A doubly linked list (see Figure 2.2) offers efficient bi-directional traversal and processing of data. The improvement is achieved by storing in each node two links to both previous and next nodes. The space cost of links and its effect on the performance are normally ignored in the initial analysis of algorithms.

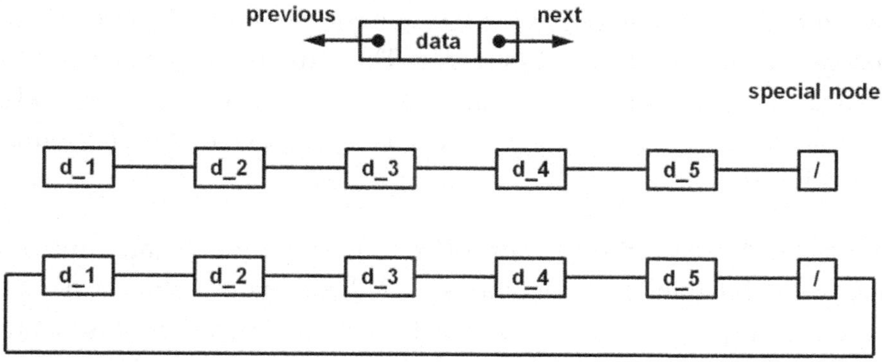

Figure 2.2: A doubly linked list that stores 5 data elements and its representation using a circular list. Each link in the list is symmetric. It depicts a pair of forward and reverse links.

The computational complexity of visiting nearest neighbour node in linked lists is constant. This cost is acceptable for many practical applications that require sequential access to a range or all of the data elements stored in a list.

In theory, linked lists have another attractive property. The computational complexity of insertion and deletion operations for a single node is constant too. In practice, however, it might not be possible to take advantage of this high efficiency, since an algorithm must reach a required node. The issue is that in liked lists access to distant elements is slow. The running time of moving to kth neighbor in these lists is $O(k)$, where k is the distance between two nodes as a number of links connecting two specified nodes.

2.1.2 Balanced Linked Trees

The linked trees are the data structures that offer substantially better performance for many applications than linked lists. The balance and more complex structure are crucial to achieving this superiority.

For any balanced tree, the performance of primary operations depends on its height, which is logarithmic in the number of nodes. The connectivity of nodes guarantees not only very fast bottom-up and top-down traversal but also very fast traversal between any two nodes in the tree. A shortest path between two nodes passes through a common parent node and only in the worst case it reaches the root of a tree. The structure of a balanced tree is optimized to avoid linear time traversal of long chains of linked nodes. In the properly designed trees, the balance is insensitive to the distribution or order of input data.

The balanced trees offer better overall performance than linked lists, despite the fact that their insertions and deletions are slower. They take logarithmic time, whereas in linked lists these operations take constant time. The use of balanced trees in applications is beneficial, because they support smaller number of inefficient primary operations. They offer much faster access to arbitrary data elements in a tree.

The obvious but interesting fact about trees is that the dramatic performance improvement (from linear to logarithmic) is achieved by the cost of adding just one link compared to doubly linked lists.

2.1.3 Complete and Perfect Binary Trees

A complete binary tree is one of the simplest non-linear structures. We define a complete binary tree as a binary tree in which each level, except the deepest, is completely filled. The deepest level is contiguously filled from left to right. If the deepest level is completely filled, the binary tree is perfect (see Figure 2.3).

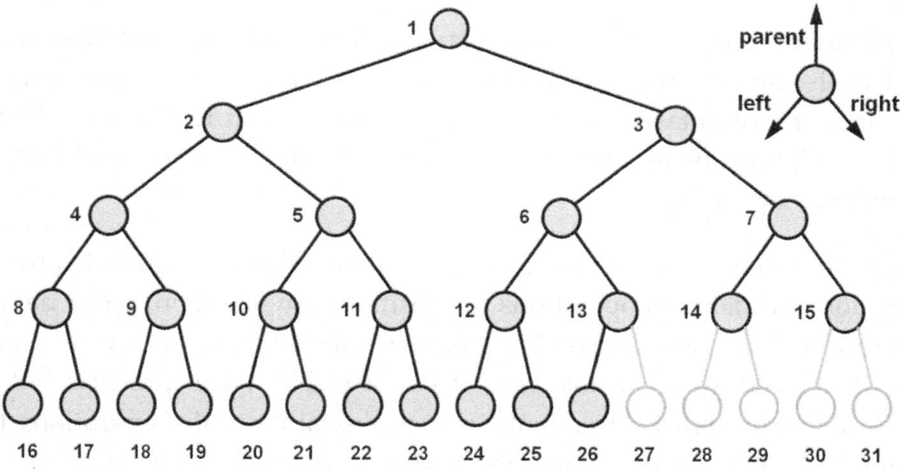

Figure 2.3: A complete binary tree that has 26 nodes (outlines in black) and a perfect binary tree with 31 nodes (additional 5 nodes are empty and have light gray outlines). The nodes are constructed and numbered in top-down and left-to-right order.

A complete binary tree is a remarkable data structure, which has interesting properties. Although it is not a general purpose data structure, its variety of fast operations is sufficient to make it very useful in such important applications as the representation of a binary heap and priority queue. The complete and perfect binary trees are also of particular importance in the context of this book.

The key feature of a heap based on a complete binary tree is the optimal use of the vertical dimension for the data arrangement. The operations that change the number of data elements in a tree take logarithmic time. The implementation of these operations is very simple, since there is no need to change connectivity of nodes in a tree, which is always balanced. In order to restore the heap order, these operations move data up or down by swapping keys and values between parent and child nodes.

The storage facilities of complete binary trees are determined by the strict rules. The position of each node in a tree does not change for the whole lifetime of the node because of the fixed structural relationships between a parent node and its children. Each internal level is filled to its maximum capacity. The deepest level can grow and contract at the right end only.

The combination of simple fixed structural relationships between nodes and well-defined storage facilities makes a complete binary tree ideal for the array representation of this data structure, which is discussed below. This is a significant advantage over other types of linked trees and lists, but it comes at the high price.

The main issue of the storage facilities is that it does not provide efficient insertion and deletion operations for positions anywhere in a user dataset. Because of this issue, adding just one new element has the computational cost of rebuilding the whole tree. It is not forbidden in practice, but the operation must not be frequent. In the general case, the operations that change the size of a user dataset stored in a complete binary tree are very expensive.

Unfortunately, this is a serious limitation to other important applications. As any other balanced tree, a complete binary tree efficiently supports search operations. Thus, it is potentially useful in processing of large datasets. However, as a search tree it does not even meet the basic requirements for the representation of a mathematical set, since its variety of efficient operations is not wide enough.

2.1.4 Search Trees

The set of efficient search, insertion and deletion operations required for processing of large datasets is supported by the balanced search trees. These trees are thoroughly covered in many textbooks. Here, we mention just a few types of them.

A binary search tree is one of the simplest data structures for efficient processing of datasets. The structure of this type of a tree is similar to that of a complete binary tree, but it is more flexible. This is why, such a tree offers much better performance of insertion and deletion operations. The main drawback of this tree is that its performance is sensitive to the data distribution in input. The binary search tree is balanced only on average. If the tree has a relatively long chain of nodes, it becomes as inefficient as a linked list. In the worst case, the performance of such a tree degrades to linear.

Both types of binary trees discussed so far are not acceptable for general applications, but the reasons are different. The structure of a complete binary tree is too rigid. It is optimal for search operations only. On the other hand, a binary search tree performs better on average, but its structure is too flexible. These facts suggest that the right degree of flexibility is in between these two extreme cases. In order to achieve logarithmic performance, which is insensitive to input, the structure of a tree does not have to be perfect. However, modifying operations on the tree must control the amount of structural defects. The balance in such a tree is not guaranteed to be perfect, but the tree gains the ability to efficiently absorb new data elements to serve client needs. As discussed earlier, logarithmic height is the key feature of a tree that supports its high efficiency. Each balanced tree implements methods that maintain the optimal height of the tree and restore structural invariants when they are violated by modifying operations. A detailed discussion of these important but difficult methods is beyond the scope of this book.

A significant downside of the imperfect structure of these trees is the loss of the benefits of the array representation of a data structure. For a particular example, refer to the discussion of a complete binary tree in Section 2.1.3 and Section 2.2.4. In addition, balanced trees have relatively complex algorithms for insertion and deletion operations. In theory, the choice between required performance and implementation complexity is a difficult one, since specific algorithms vary significantly from tree to tree. However, the variety of data structures suitable for practical applications is not so wide. One of the most popular balanced trees is a red-black tree. Its linked structure of nodes is space efficient and fine-tuned for in-memory implementations.

The significance of the following data structure is hard to overestimate. No analysis of algorithms for large datasets would be complete without a discussion of B-trees and B+-trees, which are the main data structures in database products. They are of particular interest to us too. We will use some variants of these data structures for the explanation of ideas and principles of designing new efficient algorithms. It is important to note that these data structures allow for not only on-disk but also in-memory implementations. The latter variants are normally array-based. For representing one on-disk block, these variants use a node, which has two arrays for keys and links to children nodes. It is also necessary to note that these trees have found wide application in many areas, not only databases. In particular, the in-memory B-trees and B+-trees are popular choice in the computational geometry.

In the context of processing of large datasets, a limitation of a red-black tree is associated with its small branching factor. The height of a tree grows relatively rapidly with the number of elements. A better performance is normally achieved with data structures that have smaller heights. The larger application scale, the more likely that the design decision will be in favour of B-trees or B+-trees. These trees can have a branching factor of order 100 or even 1000, which is significantly larger than in binary and red-black trees. In addition to this, the variation of this parameter allows us to control the height of a B-tree or B+-tree and fine-tune its performance for specific client needs.

2.1.5 Representation of a Sequence Using Basic Trees

In theory, a basic tree can be used to represent a mathematical sequence. This is important facility for many practical applications. However, the algorithms on trees are not as straightforward as those on linked lists. There are complications that make such a representation not practical.

The support for a sequence requires that a data structure maintain data elements in the order specified by a user algorithm and efficiently find at least a next element. The balanced search trees do not meet these requirements, because they store elements sorted by keys. These trees are suitable for sets, but not sequences. On the other hand, without sorted order balanced trees do not support efficient search operations and sequential access to distant elements has the same linear time as in linked lists. Such trees may become even slower than linked lists.

In any linked data structure, sequential processing uses a deterministic method for traversing nodes. The details of supporting algorithms depend on the structure and do not depend on data stored in the linked data structure.

The complex connectivity of a tree allows for several sequential processing methods. For example, a binary linked tree offers the following algorithms: preorder, inorder, postorder and level order traversal. The potential source of confusion and errors with these methods is that the order of visited data elements depends on the traversal algorithm. The most appropriate choice for a sequence representation is inorder traversal illustrated in Figure 2.4.

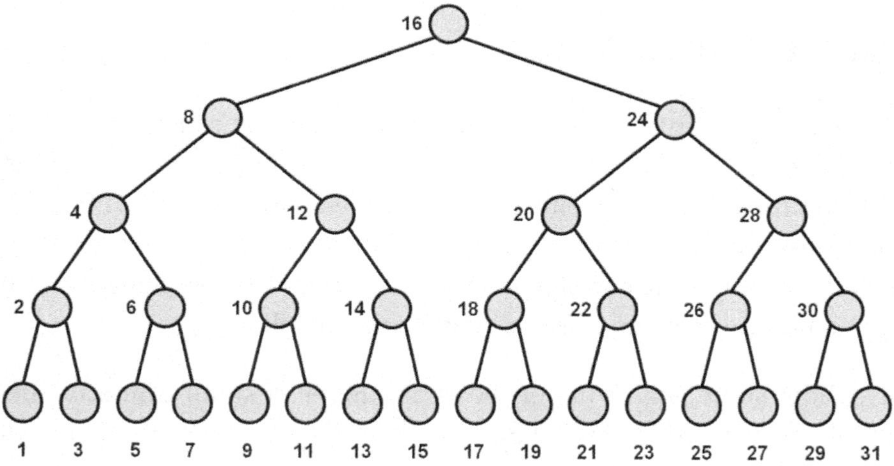

Figure 2.4: A perfect binary tree with nodes numbered by the inorder traversal algorithm. For comparison, see Figure 2.3, which numbers nodes using level order traversal.

The fundamental issue of the representation of a sequence using a tree is that it is rather mathematical than physical. The branching structure of a tree does not match the one-dimensional nature of the time. The tree structure is best suitable for modelling the spatial arrangement of objects. Any linear structure does not have this issue, since it is one-dimensional and it has one degree of freedom. It stores data with a one-to-one correspondence between an element position and a time point. In terms of a physical approach, a singly linked list is the best abstraction to model the irreversible nature of the time.

Generally, it would not make sense to discuss the representation of a mathematical sequence using a linked tree. In textbooks, this aspect of trees is normally omitted. The representation is not absolutely useless, but a tree is the least suitable basic data structure for the task and its use is error prone. It may look surprising at this stage that we consider this option at all. However, as we will see later, the balanced trees have significant potential for improving performance of primary operations. With the method of augmenting a basic tree can be transformed into an advanced data structure. The performance gain is so dramatic that the enhanced tree can replace arrays in many important large scale applications.

2.2 PROPERTIES OF ARRAYS

Arrays have quite interesting and unusual properties compared to linked data structures. On the one hand, the ease of using arrays allows us to quickly write code for algorithms, but simple array-based solutions often cause serious performance problems. On the other hand, arrays can help us to develop highly efficient algorithms, but it might be challenging to find the right method of using them to achieve this result.

Arrays, both static and dynamic, have a number of significant advantages over linked data structures. They offer better space efficiency and better performance of several primary operations. As a sequence, an array can easily outperform a singly or doubly linked list. Arrays are a good choice in many practical applications of small to medium scale. For these reasons, in the C++ standard library `std::vector<T>`, which implements a dynamic array, is a default container.

In textbooks, arrays are normally introduced before linked data structures, because they are directly supported by programming languages. The main aspect of an array, which is discussed in the introduction to this data structure, is the representation of a sequence through the subscript operator.

This is an important facility of arrays, but not the only one. The introductory description of arrays does not reveal the full computing power of these data structures, which offer quite a wide set of efficient facilities for user algorithms. For this reason, we briefly consider several aspects of arrays below.

As discussed in Chapter 1, we normally use the random-access machine model, which does not take advantage of locality of reference to data and guarantees constant time access to any element in an array. This theoretical model reflects one of the key features of arrays that gives them a number of advantages over linked data structures.

2.2.1 Access to *k*th Neighbour

A linked list supports only sequential access to elements. Access to a neighbour has linear running time in the number of links between origin and destination nodes. This is a potential performance bottleneck in algorithms that require frequent access to distant elements. In an array, the running time of the same operation is constant. This is the best possible performance.

2.2.2 Connectivity

The fact that any distant neighbour in an array can be reached in constant time has also the following important structural aspect. In terms of connectivity, it means that each element of an array has an implicit link to any other element in the array. An array provides quadratic number of such links without incurring space overhead. This is an important advantage over linked data structures, such as lists and trees, which may use significant amount of space to store links between nodes and guarantee constant time access to the nearest nodes only.

An array can represent a linear data structure and, thus, a sequence. However, an array does not have the constraint of one-dimensional step-by-step traversal as a linked list. This property is exploited in implicit array representations of various data structures.

2.2.3 Storage Facilities

Since an array provides a contiguous region of memory with efficient access to any address, it is very attractive to replace a system memory management. After allocation, the array is treated as raw uninitialized memory partitioned into cells of equal size. A custom memory manager uses this memory region to implement a method of storing objects in the array cells. These facilities are useful in achieving the high performance of algorithms, but this is not a trivial task.

In the context of this section, the distinctive feature of a sequence is a contiguous arrangement of elements stored in cells of an array. The insertion and deletion operations move elements between cells to keep this sequence representation valid. In the general case, both of these operations take linear time, they are too slow to support the most efficient algorithms.

The key difference of a custom memory management is that it does not move elements at all in order to avoid this inefficiency. The position of an element in an array is fixed for the whole lifetime of the element.

In simple algorithms, an array is used as a stack. These algorithms require only two operations: append a new element to the end of an array and remove the last element from the array. The next level of complexity is an array-based memory manager. When a client inserts or deletes elements, the memory manager marks array cells if they are in use or not. The custom memory management is very efficient, when all of the special operations take constant time.

The C++ standard library generalizes resources management through the concept of an allocator. A custom array-based memory manager, such as an allocator in C++, can improve performance of standard containers based on linked data structures of lists and a red-black tree. However, the use of an array in a custom memory manager does not convert a linked data structure into an array-based variant of this data structure. The space requirement remains the same due to the need for storing links and all of the implementation algorithms use these links. This use of arrays is different from the array representation of a complete binary tree that does not store any links at all (see the next Section 2.2.4).

In programming languages that do not support pointers, the storage facilities of arrays are useful to implement linked lists. The array cells store nodes of a linked data structure and indices to the array cells replace pointer based links to the nodes.

2.2.4 Array-Based Data Structures

The simple uses of arrays in data processing are based on storage facilities. For example, an array with its fast access to data, as a table of a function, can save a considerable amount of time by storing results of costly computations. The representation of a sequence is also simple, because this is essentially a built-in functionality of an array.

The advanced applications of arrays are non-trivial, but they deliver significant performance improvements. The interesting aspect of an array is that it offers efficient facilities for not only linear, but also non-linear structures. For this reason, an array is a remarkable basic data structure, which can support other types of data structures. In this section, we briefly discuss several well-known and relatively simple examples that demonstrate how to take advantage of these facilities to develop array-based data structures that offer performance better than link-based variants of the same data structures.

An array-based variant of a data structure provides a guarantee to a user that interface facilities are the same as those in a matching link-based variant. Although implementation details may differ quite significantly, an array representation is impossible without knowledge of structural relationships and invariants of the original link-based data structure.

In all of these examples, the high performance is achieved by using the same method of fast access to data in appropriate cells. Instead of a link-based search for a datum, this method simply computes the position of a required cell. An array-based data structure using this method has two advantages over an equivalent linked data structure. It is more space efficient, because it does not store links. It is also more time efficient, since the computation of a position is normally a constant time operation, whereas an efficient search on a linked data structure, such as a balanced tree, takes logarithmic time. For these reasons, the overall performance improvement can be quite substantial. This method is important for the array-based variants of algorithms that we consider later in this book.

Complete Binary Tree

The array representation of a complete binary tree is a classical example of using an array to deliver the functionality of a linked data structure of nodes with improved space and time efficiency. As mentioned in Section 2.1.3, the simple and immutable structure of a complete binary tree make it ideal for the array implementation.

The space required to store links can be saved if we provide a method for fast locating a cell matching a node in a linked tree. The method enables a client to traverse the tree as if it follows links. Assuming that the root of a tree is stored at the position 1, a client can access in constant time each node linked to the node at the position `k` through the computation of the position of a required node:

```
parent = k/2;
child_left = 2*k;
child_right = 2*k+1;
```

Saving three links per each data element is a considerable improvement, especially for small size keys. The important feature of this representation is that the array-based complete binary tree has no space overhead. Note also that the representation array provides the efficient memory management for a complete binary tree by the use of stack operations.

In modern programming languages, there is no need to implement a complete binary tree as a linked data structure of nodes, since it is less time and space efficient. However, the array representation is implicit. It may appear to be more challenging and less useful at the design stage.

Deque (Double-Ended Queue)

To clarify the discussion, a deque is not regarded as a container. Here, we define a deque as a linear structure, which supports efficient, ideally, constant time operations on both ends. Such a deque can be implemented with a doubly linked list.

The straightforward array implementation of a deque does not meet these requirements, since only the tail of a collection can be processed efficiently. The insertion and deletion operations on the head take linear running time in the number of elements in the collection.

Despite this obstacle, an efficient array-based deque is still possible. The trick is to use an array as a circular storage. The connectivity of cells in the representation array makes both ends of a deque equally open and accessible.

The high performance is achieved through the simple computation of head and tail positions of a deque in the underlying array.

Hashed Containers

Hash tables is one of the most advanced examples of using arrays as a storage. Although not all variants of these data structures are entirely array-based, the main idea is basically the same as that in the examples discussed earlier. A hash table uses an algorithm that maps a key to a position in an array.

With the properly selected hash function, these data structures support a number of constant time primary operations, which are required for the representation of sets and maps. The fast access to data elements in an array is crucial to the high performance of hash tables. The facilities of hash tables are somewhat limited due to the loss of order, but their undeniable high performance is a significant factor to consider replacing balanced search trees in practical applications, which require operations with running time better than logarithmic.

2.2.5 Algorithms on Arrays

The benefits of using arrays in programming solutions increase not only because of the significant progress in the computer hardware. The other important reason why they become more and more useful is the constant growth of the number of efficient algorithms on them. Many algorithms are highly efficient on arrays only. Their variants on linked data structures, such as lists, can be extremely slow. This fact gives arrays the big advantage over linked data structures and allows arrays to compete with balanced trees in suitable applications.

In this section, we concentrate mainly on array facilities for the representation of a mathematical set, since an array is an efficient sequence by design. For these applications, arrays offer a very wide variety of sorting and searching algorithms, which have different implementation complexity and performance guarantees. Simple and easy to implement algorithms usually take linear running time. Logarithmic time algorithms are more challenging, but they have been thoroughly studied and their performance properties are well known.

Despite linear running time of insertion and deletion operations for single elements, the pair of fast sort and search algorithms is an excellent combination to implement relatively efficient and simple representation of a mathematical set, which is suitable for small to medium scale applications. The main issue of such a representation is that its overall performance depends on the frequency of operations that change the size of a dataset.

Efficient processing of datasets requires the representation array to be ordered. For the initial construction of the array from a given dataset, there are many efficient sorting algorithms, such as quicksort or mergesort. As for searching algorithms, the choice is limited. Binary search is the general purpose algorithm, which guarantees logarithmic performance. Interpolation search is more efficient, but only if input data have a suitable distribution of keys.

2.2.6 Locality of Reference

Although we are interested in large scale applications and system specific approaches are out of scope of this book, we cannot ignore the efficiency of arrays in small scale applications.

Locality of reference is the name of a technical term. In a simplified form, it can be regarded as the compactness or density of filling array cells with useful data elements. The ideal is a contiguous storage. The greater the number of unused cells between first and last elements, the worse locality of reference.

Most modern computer systems have several types of physical memory with different efficiency of access to data: the faster memory, the smaller its size. This is a serious complication for theoretical models of computations, because the computational complexity of an algorithm depends of the problem size and its asymptotic value is valid for the largest and slowest memory. In contrast, the optimized algorithms take advantage of the smallest and fastest computer memory.

The big advantage of arrays over dynamically allocated linked data structures is that arrays maximize the space efficiency by storing data elements in contiguous memory regions. The array-based variants of data structures offer the additional performance improvement, when they store only data elements and do not store links.

The efficiency of primary operations on arrays is so high that for an acceptable practical representation it is often sufficient to use simple and in theory slow algorithms, such as insertion sort and sequential search. In addition, there is no need to worry about whether data are ordered or not. We can fine-tune such a representation and satisfy the performance requirements at the last stages of the development.

The strength of arrays in small scale applications is very important for the development of large complex data structures, which use arrays as basic building blocks. A good example of such a complex data structure is an array-based B+ tree (see Section 2.6 and Section 3.13).

2.2.7 Limitations

An array is a powerful data structure, which is superior to other basic data structures in many applications. Despite this fact, an array, as a single type of a data structure, is not sufficient to address all of the computational challenges in processing of large datasets. It has significant issues of space and time efficiency that limit its application area.

Insertion and Deletion

It is well known that because of contiguous arrangement, in a typical application using an array inserting and deleting a single element takes linear running time, except for positions near the tail of the data storage.

In theory, this is not a problem, since there are no performance restrictions on operations of a set and a sequence in the mathematical definition of these abstract concepts. An operation is either allowed or not. Unfortunately, in practical applications, the situation is different. A computer representation of a mathematical concept is required to be efficient and the linear time performance of insertions and deletions is generally unacceptable for processing of large datasets.

This inefficiency is a fundamental problem. The contiguous arrangement of elements is quite important for practical applications of arrays, since it is nearly perfect for implementing a sequence. It offers the advantages of simple code and high performance due to maximized locality of reference.

One of the approaches to deal with this performance problem is to use the efficient memory management facilities of arrays that avoid moving a large number of elements when a dataset is modified, see Section 2.2.3 for a discussion. This approach is good enough, since the mathematical definition of a sequence and, thus, sequential processing do not require data to be stored contiguously in an array. However, losing benefits of the performance associated with locality of reference and the simplicity of code can be a significant factor for some algorithms. In some applications, it is also possible to avoid moving elements by using swap operations.

The advanced data structures offer the general approach to implementing efficient insertion and deletion operations of a sequence. This is one of the topics of this book, which we cover in Chapter 3.

Space Efficiency

A static array is a good choice only when the size of a user dataset has been specified at the development time. In the ideal use case, the dataset is not modified after initialization. However, in the real world applications, a user input is rarely so trivial. Normally, the size of a user dataset, its dynamics (how it changes over time) and its data distribution are either vaguely specified or vary widely. This is why, there are many significant challenges to address in the applications. The development of efficient algorithms requires thorough analysis and design to guarantee the worst case performance. For such inputs, a static array is no longer a good choice, since it has no flexibility. In order to meet the best performance requirements, it must reserve the maximum number of cells. However, it is likely that only small number of them will be filled with useful data at run time.

A dynamic array offers much better solution to the problem of allocating the optimal amount of memory for datasets that can grow and shrink. In order to avoid significant waste of space it doubles the capacity of the array. This method works well in many applications, but it is not suitable for large datasets. It is not safe, since simple doubling the capacity can crash an application. In addition, slow insertion and deletion operations on large arrays will cause serious degradation in the overall performance.

Dynamic memory allocation has been designed and added to programming languages to address the non-trivial challenges of dealing with various types of user inputs. Memory management is based on the most advanced algorithms. For this reason, dynamically allocated data structures offer a greater degree of flexibility than arrays for handling frequent modifications of datasets.

Another aspect of the space inefficiency of arrays is associated with imperfect data distribution in practical applications. A simple example is a sparse array, which, by definition, has a huge size and stores only a small number of non-zero keys and/or values. All other data elements are unnecessary in the application domain. Using a normal array to store a huge number of useless data elements is a significant waste of expensive computer memory. A linked list might be more suitable for the representation of such a sparse array. In the general case, choosing or developing the optimal representation for a sparse array is not a trivial problem.

In the real world applications, the problems like this one are even more challenging to address because of the difference in the memory size of original data elements. The sparse array is a simplified approximate model of a dataset that contains mainly small values that do not use many bits in the binary representation. At the same time, the type of a data element must have enough bits to save with high precision large values, which are not frequent. If the small values are significant and cannot be discarded, the problem cannot be reduced to the sparse array problem. Using compression methods is not always possible, since they adversely affect the overall performance. In this case, the loss of space is unavoidable. When parameters and properties of an input dataset vary in wide ranges, the straightforward use of arrays to store and process large datasets is unlikely to deliver time and space efficient solution.

2.3 DATA SCHEMES FOR BASIC DATA STRUCTURES

A data scheme can be regarded as a method of data organization in the storage provided by a structure of linked nodes or array cells. For a given structured storage, there are many ways to fill in memory regions of nodes or cells, but not all of them are effective. The best combinations of structures and data schemes produce classical data structures. We already discussed several specific data schemes in the examples of basic data structures. Here, we will summarize important aspects of using data schemes for performance optimization. The aspect of applications of data schemes is left for other sections that consider entire data structures.

The importance of data arrangement is obvious from the simple consideration. If we arbitrarily or randomly place data elements in the storage provided by a data structure, we will lose the efficiency of data analysis, since in this case we can use only the least efficient sequential search. The correct choice of a data scheme allows us to achieve the best possible performance of operations required in a user application.

2.3.1 Linear Data Structures

The data schemes for linear data structures are trivial, compared to more complex data structures. The linked lists and array-based sequences can support only two data schemes to store either ordered or unordered datasets.

Although for linked lists there is no restriction on a data scheme, using ordered linked lists in some applications may appear to be impractical. The order preserving operations are generally slow due to linear time access to distant elements.

2.3.2 Arrays as Sequences

Unlike linked lists, both ordered and unordered arrays are widely used in applications. Arrays have the advantage of very fast constant time access to data elements. Because of this property, arrays offer many useful and efficient sorting algorithms to prepare data for subsequent processing. The ordered arrays offer additional performance benefits, since they support efficient search algorithms, such as binary search on keys or values, which are significantly faster than sequential search. These advantages of ordered arrays are particularly important in practical applications.

2.3.3 Array-Based Storage and Data Structures

Since a data scheme is normally independent of a data structure representation, all other applications of arrays do not require a separate analysis. When an array serves as a storage, the analysis of a data scheme is reduced to that of a linked data structure, which is stored in the array. As for array-based data structures, they implicitly support the same data schemes as link-based variants support explicitly. Thus, it is sufficient to consider data schemes of matching linked data structures.

2.3.4 Trees

The trees support a number of potentially useful options to arrange data elements, because their structure is not linear. The trees have both horizontal and vertical dimensions to arrange elements in nodes. The second dimension allows for data schemes that are not possible in linear structures. The interesting design question is how to take advantage of the vertical dimension to achieve the best performance of tree operations.

A bright example of the optimal use of the vertical dimension is a binary heap, which is based on a complete binary tree (see Figure 2.3). At the same time, it is well known that a binary tree can be used with another data scheme, which can be regarded as orthogonal (see Figure 2.5). The resulting data structure is a binary search tree. The two data structures use the same type of a binary tree but different data schemes and, thus, guarantee the high performance of different primary operations. This simple comparison shows how we can obtain data structures for different purposes by changing the data scheme.

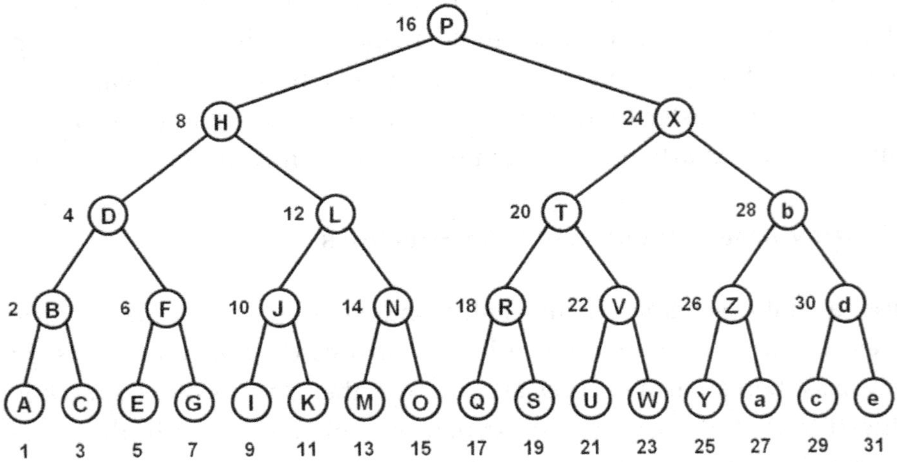

Figure 2.5: A binary search trees with the space optimal data scheme. Each node stores a unique element of a given dataset.

The data scheme of a binary search tree shown in Figure 2.5 is the main data scheme of balanced search trees, which is considered in many textbooks on data structures and algorithms. In this scheme, ordering restrictions are applied to the horizontal dimension only. The vertical dimension of a tree is used for fast top-down search. The number of nodes in such a search tree is equal to the number of elements in a user dataset. Thus, the important advantage of this data scheme is that it is space optimized. It is ideal for dynamically allocated data structures, which avoid allocating system resources in advance for new data to be added to the user dataset.

The disadvantages of trees may result from their complex structure. It affects the implementation of primary operations, such as insertion and deletion, and even the simplest traversal algorithms for sequential processing are not completely trivial on trees. Compared to linked lists, the structural complexity makes trees more difficult for the design of the optimal data scheme, which serves all of the primary operations and internal algorithms.

Despite a number of advantages, this space optimal data scheme for search trees is not always the best choice in large scale applications. This is why, we briefly describe the idea of another data scheme. We begin with a simple variant and continue the discussion of specific details of this data scheme in further sections.

The key feature of this data scheme is that it stores all of the elements of a user dataset in leaf nodes. In basic variants, the internal nodes store only keys. The structure of internal nodes represents a sub-tree, which is used

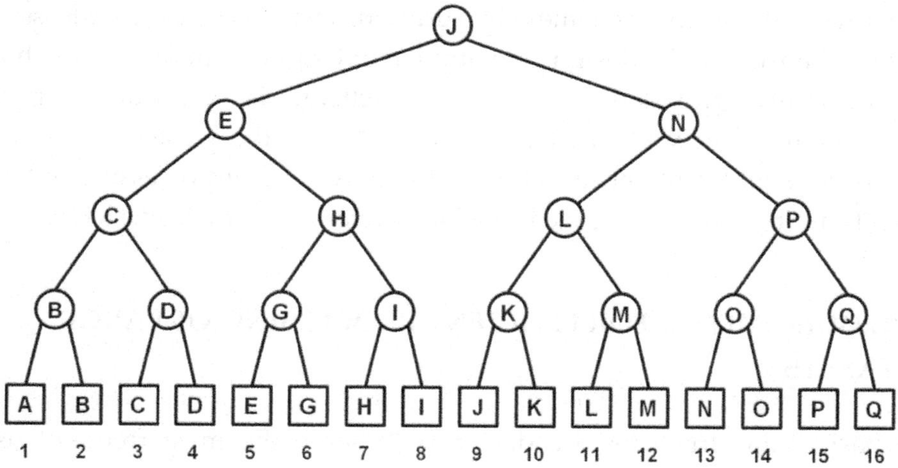

Figure 2.6: A binary search tree with the data scheme that stores a given dataset in external nodes and allows for duplicate keys in internal nodes. Note that the same total number of nodes as in Figure 2.5 provides storage for only 16 data elements instead of 31.

for the efficient navigation similar to that in any other type of search trees. The search starts at the root and terminates at a leaf regardless of whether it is a search hit or miss. Although the length of a search path is logarithmic in the size of a user dataset, on average it is longer than in a search tree with the space optimized data scheme, where a search hit can occur before reaching a leaf node.

At this stage it may appear a bit strange that we are interested in a data scheme that allows us to store redundant data, waste space and complicate the entire data structure. The significant benefits of this data scheme will become clear when we start fine-tuning this data scheme for processing of large datasets. For now, we highlight the following properties of this scheme. Unlike the standard space efficient data scheme of search trees, the alternative scheme is essentially based on two types of nodes. A user algorithm can take advantage of associating different information with internal and external nodes. In advanced variants, the internal nodes can store not only keys but also any other data that help improve performance of user algorithms. This facility enables us to implement more than one data scheme using one structure of nodes. A method using such a complex data scheme is more space efficient than a method using several data structures with simple schemes. In addition, fast access to a wide set of various data can help design and implement more complex algorithms. The flexibility provided by this data scheme is important for the development of new efficient algorithms. As for the wasted space, this issue is not significant because the most widely used in processing of large datasets are B+-trees with large branching factors and small size keys.

2.4 REQUIREMENTS FOR EFFICIENT PROCESSING OF LARGE DATASETS

The basic data structures are designed to serve the most frequent user needs for information processing. In most practical applications, a user constructs and modifies a dataset with insertion and deletion operations and uses search operations for analysis and modelling. In some applications, data are only accumulated and never deleted. Each data element might be a valuable piece of information due to a high cost of obtaining the data. The other reason is that the complete original dataset might be used in the future to build a new mathematical or business model.

The two fundamental mathematical concepts widely used in computer science and programming solutions are a set and a sequence. We begin with a discussion of basic data structures that can represent a set. In order to meet the simple requirements discussed above, a data structure is expected to support the following three operations: search, insertion and deletion. Efficient processing of large datasets requires that each of these operations take at most logarithmic time. This performance should not depend on the distribution of data in a user input.

The following table shows the computational complexities of primary operations of several basic data structures that we briefly discussed so far.

	Unordered List	Ordered List	Unordered Array	Ordered Array	Red-Black Tree
Search	$O(N)$	$O(N)$	$O(N)$	$O(\log N)$	$O(\log N)$
Insertion	$O(1)$	$O(1)$	$O(N)$	$O(N)$	$O(\log N)$
Deletion	$O(1)$	$O(1)$	$O(N)$	$O(N)$	$O(\log N)$

Table 2.1: The computational complexities of primary operations of representations of a mathematical set using basic data structures. Linked list and unordered array use sequential search, ordered array uses binary search. N is the number of elements in a given dataset.

The performance of specific operations in this table shows that the best basic data structure, which meets these criteria, is a balanced search tree. Because of high efficiency of all of its primary operations, it is also the best general purpose data structure for the specified application.

In theory, the second best data structure is an ordered array with binary search. However, it is often the first choice for small datasets, since it can outperform dynamically allocated trees. As a dataset grows, linear time of insertions and deletions becomes a significant problem. At some point, a user algorithm may replace the representation with a more efficient one.

Linked lists are not practical even for small sets, no matter how fast their insertion and deletion operations. They have been included mainly for comparison of basic data structures.

The important fact about Table 2.1 is that most of the representations of a set provide both fast and slow operations. The main concern is operations that take linear time, since they are potential performance bottlenecks. This is a significant complication for using basic data structures in practical applications, since the choice based on theoretical analysis is not always the best for specific computer systems.

The algorithmic solutions to complex practical problems involve many primary operations that are ideally provided by one data structure. For example, a typical data processing application finds an appropriate position in a dataset and then inserts a new data element into the dataset. The two primary operations of search and insertion support incremental construction of a dataset to be used for information retrieval. If at least one of these primary operations is slow the overall performance of processing drops dramatically.

One of the objectives of this book is to describe methods that enable us to address this performance problem of complex algorithms by creating data structures that extend the variety of efficient primary operations. This can be achieved with an improvement in performance of existing operations or with the development of new operations. It is often possible to develop a data structure that has no one inefficient operation in the client domain. However, before we go into detail, let us examine the requirements for practical applications in a broader context.

2.5 RANGE QUERIES

The analysis of minimal requirements for efficient processing of large datasets leads us to the conclusion that the implementation of a mathematical set would be a good start for the development of the general purpose methods. A set is a very powerful abstraction, which is useful in numerous practical applications. But is it all we need? Is it sufficient to cover a wide area of applications of large datasets?

One of the strengths of a computer representation of a set is that it provides very efficient operations to test if data contain a specific element or not. Normally, such an operation returns a Boolean value of ***true*** or ***false***. In terms of the number of occurrences of the specific element, the result is either 0 or 1. However, the data analysis in many practical applications requires more than a search for a single element. If a dataset is large, say, millions or billions of elements, the difference of one element is not significant to affect the correctness of data analysis.

Instead of single elements, the analysis of large datasets concentrates on groups of elements with similar or close properties, such as clusters. The sizes of such groups are important pieces of information for solving a user problem. These sizes are extensions of 0 and 1 counts in the pure set-based analysis of data. As a dataset grows, instead of ***contains or not,*** it becomes more important and useful to know ***how many***.

The range queries are designed to analyze large datasets using the partition of a key space. A group of elements in a range can be identified using a comparison operation provided by a client. Note the high level of the generality of this method of analysis, which is both the strength and the weakness in applications. The method of partition does not require the key space to support a metric or a distance function between two elements. With such a query, a client can obtain the number of elements and/or a subset of elements in a specified range.

In data analysis, the range queries are as fundamental as finding minimum and maximum values of a function. The range queries enable a user to understand the distribution of data and make appropriate decisions. The number of elements in a specified range enables a user to avoid costly computations that involve processing of each element in the range. Thus, the performance of this range query is of particular practical importance.

In theory, the ***contains*** operation of a set can help answer a range query though testing each possible ***key*** space point in the given range, but this method is not practical. It is extremely inefficient due to potentially huge number of points to be tested.

This brief discussion leads us to the conclusion that in order to make our data structures useful in practical analysis and modelling, the requirements for efficient processing of large datasets should be extended to cover range queries. A set-based analysis of large datasets is both simplistic and inefficient to answer such queries. Thus, a suitable data structure should provide special high performance operations and algorithms that support range queries.

In terms of mathematical concepts, a group of elements in a range is frequently regarded as a subset. However, for the implementation of efficient range queries algorithms, it is more convenient to view the group as a smaller size sequence obtained from a given sequence. This approach allows us to use simple and efficient algorithms of counting and reporting elements between two specified positions in the original sequence. This fact suggests that in order to satisfy the new extended requirements, which include range queries, a suitable data structure must efficiently represent not only a mathematical set, but also a mathematical sequence.

The combination of facilities of two mathematical concepts is an interesting and important aspect of using data structures and algorithms in practical applications. A data structure that represents only one mathematical concept is often not sufficient to solve problems or serve needs of clients that require a wide variety of efficient operations or facilities in their application domains. At the same time, the variety should not be too wide to avoid rarely used operations. The complexity and diversity of the real world applications is one of the main challenges for the design of useful general purpose libraries of data structures and algorithms.

The new requirement for range queries is an important reason to re-consider the performance of basic data structures. So far, we have found that the best basic data structure for processing of large datasets is a balanced search tree, such as a red-black tree. The conclusion is based on the performance of its facilities for the general purpose representation of a set. Now, it is essential that a data structure provides efficient facilities of a sequence too.

As discussed in Section 2.1.5, a balanced tree can support a sequence, but it is not the best and very unusual choice in practice for a number of reasons. A binary search tree or red-black tree supports range queries through search and inorder traversal of a tree, which is an algorithm of sequential processing similar to that in linear data structures. Because of search for end positions of a range, this algorithm takes time at least logarithmic in the total number of elements or linear in the height of a tree regardless of the distance between first and last elements in a range. When the number of elements in a specified range is small compared to the height of a tree, the search operations take significant amount of time.

Another issue is caused by the complexity of up and down traversal of a tree, which is used to find and report all of the elements in a range. Similar algorithms on linked lists are very simple because one link connects two nodes with two consecutive elements. The structure of a tree has the interesting property that sequentially ordered current and next elements of a range can be stored in nodes that are not connected by one link. In the worst case (see Figure 2.7), the length of a path connecting two nodes with two consecutive elements is proportional to the tree height.

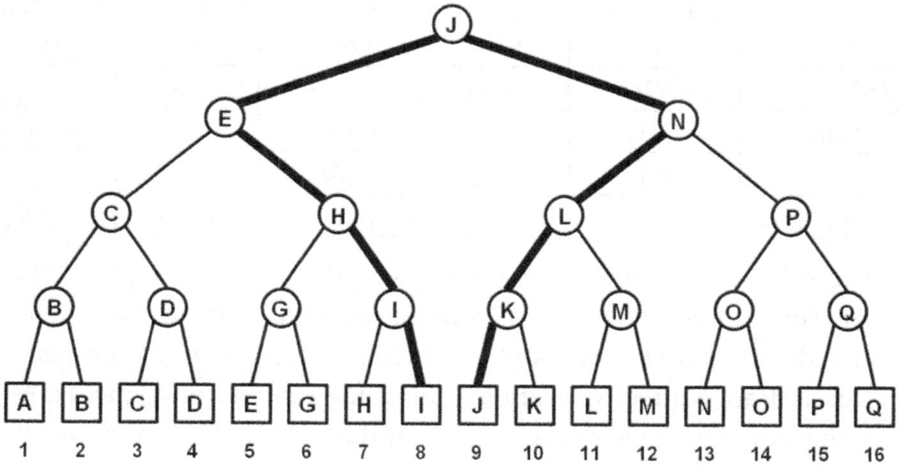

Figure 2.7: A path connecting two consecutive data elements (eighth and ninth) that passes through the root of a balanced binary tree.

The performance of range queries on red-black trees is not perfect but acceptable for many applications that require a wide variety of efficient primary operations. For comparison, a hash table, which offers faster search operations, cannot replace a red-black tree in such applications, because it does not support range queries. The last fact explains why hash tables and hashing algorithms are not in the main focus of this book. On the other hand, since facilities of a red-black tree for sequential processing are sub-optimal, it makes sense to examine other data structures in the context of requirements for range queries.

Linked lists and arrays are the fundamental data structures designed for the best possible computer representation of a mathematical sequence. Not surprisingly, these data structures are superior to trees in terms of facilities for range queries. A linked list has the significant advantage of the optimal connectivity of nodes. Both reporting and counting elements are straightforward algorithms that take time linear in the number of elements in a range. An array is even better basic data structure for range queries due to fast access to arbitrary positions. In an array, counting the number of elements in a range is a constant time operation.

	Unordered List	Ordered List	Unordered Array	Ordered Array	Red-Black Tree
Search	$O(N)$	$O(N)$	$O(N)$	$O(\log N)$	$O(\log N)$
Insertion	$O(1)$	$O(1)$	$O(N)$	$O(N)$	$O(\log N)$
Deletion	$O(1)$	$O(1)$	$O(N)$	$O(N)$	$O(\log N)$
Range Query	$O(N)$	$O(K)$	$O(N)$	$O(1)$	$O(K)$

Table 2.2: The computational complexities of primary operations for set representations and range queries. Linked lists and unordered array use sequential search, ordered array uses binary search. Range query operation - count the number of elements. ***N*** is the number of elements in a given dataset. ***K*** is the number of elements in a range.

This discussion shows that there are two types of data structures that offer efficient facilities for different mathematical concepts: a balanced search tree for a set and a linear data structure (list or array) for a sequence. This is a usual problem with basic data structures. Many practical solutions are based on several data structures representing different mathematical concepts, since they do not have a better choice. Such solutions are often acceptable, but they are not optimal. For the best performance, we should use one data structure with the set of all of the required fast operations.

Our list does not yet include a data structure that meets new extended requirements by offering the advantages of two types of basic data structures. In order to find an improvement, it would be reasonable to ask, for example, the following question:

Is it possible to design a data structure that takes advantage of two data structures: a balanced search tree and a linked list?

It appears that this is not only possible, but this is also one of the most effective methods of achieving desired performance of a data structure in a user application.

2.6 B+-TREES

The well-known example of using this design method is a B+-tree, which represents a modified structural variant of a B-tree. Visually, a B+-tree consists of two connected basic data structures of a B-tree and a linked list. A B-tree stores only keys and a linked list at the deepest level stores all of the elements of a user dataset. Note that there is no restriction on the type of a linked list. Both singly and doubly linked lists can be used at the deepest level of a B+-tree.

Such a complex data structure offers all of the advantages of a balanced search tree and a linked list. It supports efficient search operations on keys and, because it supports sequential processing with the efficiency of a linked list, it addresses the performance issue of range queries on a B-tree.

It is interesting to note that originally B+-trees were developed not for the reason of structural issues that we discussed above for the balanced search trees. The main problem of original on-disk B-trees is the inefficiency of sequential processing and range queries due to visiting nodes at different levels. The algorithms, which cross levels in these trees, are very costly for the overall performance because of huge difference in access time between the disks and RAM. However, the method of solving the original problem is general. It is applicable to in-memory data structures too. The example of a B+-tree is particularly useful in the context of this book, since this data structure is optimized for large scale applications.

The design of B+-trees shows how to address the challenges of complex requirements of practical applications. When none of basic data structures is suitable, we design a new data structure that has the connectivity to efficiently support operations required in a user domain. The complexity of a data structure that supports a wide variety of efficient primary operations only mirrors the complexity of an application area. The comparative analysis of B+-trees and B-trees is one of the brightest examples for learning and understanding methods of the design useful data structures for large datasets.

A complex data structure is designed to support the most efficient facilities of all of the basic data structure involved. It can be implemented using a union of sets of nodes and links of basic data structures. A basic algorithm on such a complex structure uses a sub-structure of nodes and links. For a B+-tree, a data structure obtained after such set operations can be illustrated with the arithmetic operation:

B+-tree = B-tree + list

This simple formula explains the origin of '+' in the name of a B+-tree.

It is important to note that the complex connectivity of a new data structure changes its classification type. Strictly and formally speaking, the new complex data structure is a graph that supports efficient primary operations of its basic data structures. In the case of a B+-tree, these are a search tree and a linked list. Because of this structural complexity, a B+-tree is different from a typical tree, such as a basic balanced tree.

2.7 LEVEL LINKED DATA STRUCTURES

A B+-tree improves the performance of sequential processing and range queries of an original B-tree by linking nodes at the deepest level. We illustrate the idea of designing a B+-tree with a balanced binary tree (see Figure 2.8). This tree uses the data scheme, which stores elements of a user dataset in nodes of the deepest level, since this is the standard choice for B+-trees. The deepest level of this modified structure now represents a simple linked list, which offers efficient operations for sequential processing and range queries. This list helps us to avoid using costly operations of the basic binary tree that search through high levels and the root of the tree.

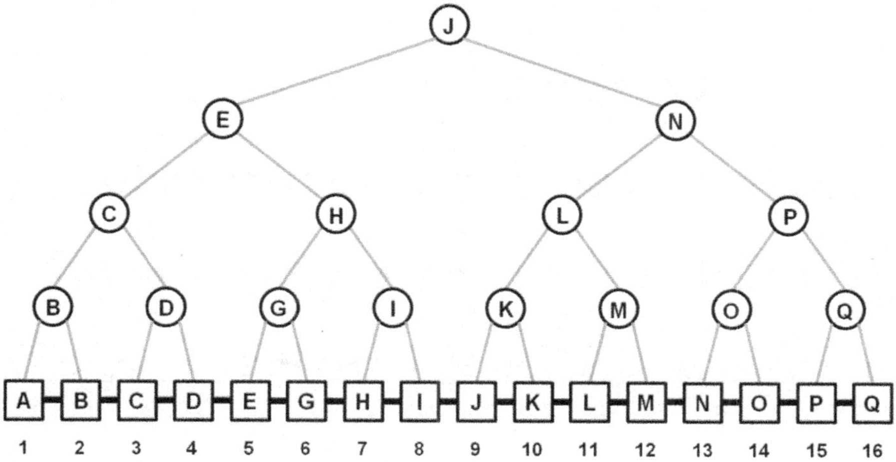

Figure 2.8: A balanced binary tree with the data scheme and connectivity of nodes of a search B+-tree. The deepest level of the tree represents a linked list, which stores all of the elements of a given dataset.

The performance improvement achieved by modifying connectivity of the deepest level of the tree suggests the following enhancement of the structure. If we now have a look at the next level above the deepest one, we will find that adjacent nodes of this level are not connected. It means that this data structure has the same problem of sub-optimal sequential access to distant nodes for the second lowest level of the tree. The main method is to move up to the root and then down as in a basic balanced tree. The other method is to move down, go through nodes of the deepest level and then move up, but this is efficient only for relatively close neighbors. The solution to this problem is straightforward. We apply the same method that has been used for the deepest level in order to connect nodes of the second level in a linked list. If we now continue this procedure for each level up, we will obtain a level linked variant of the original basic tree (see Figure 2.9).

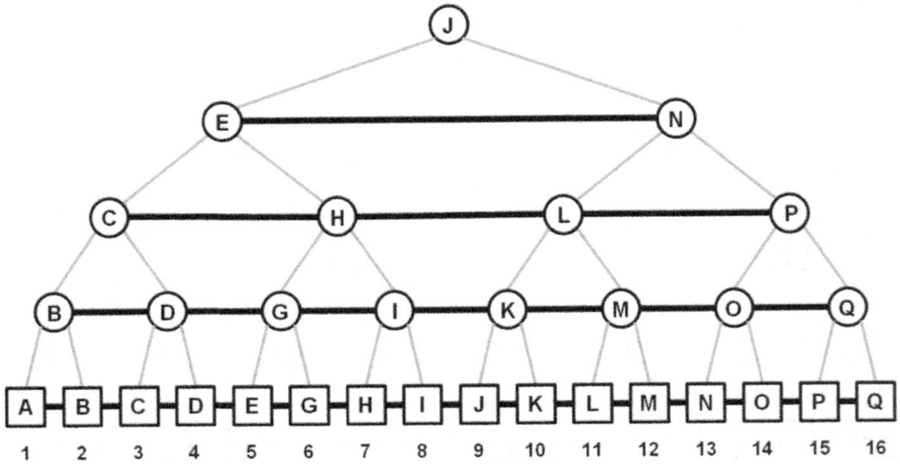

Figure 2.9: A level linked variant of the binary tree shown in Figure 2.8. Each level of the tree represents a linked list. A user dataset is stored in nodes of the deepest level.

The benefits of a level linked structure are more significant than addressing the performance issue of range queries. Linking nodes at all of the levels of this structure widens the choice of nodes and links in finding an optimal path between two given nodes. The rich connectivity enables local searches that avoid or minimize the frequency of costly visits of the root of the tree. One of the most useful algorithms is known as finger search. For not quite distant nodes, it is more efficient than the standard top-down search, since its running time is logarithmic in the number of elements in a given range, instead of the total number of elements in a dataset. Another important advantage over basic trees is efficient sequential processing of data at each level. The level-linked structures also preserve the functionality of original basic trees. The efficient algorithms on a tree, which pass through the root, have the same implementation and are available for client tasks.

2.8 COMPARISON BASED AND DISTANCE BASED DATA SCHEMES

As discussed above, the general purpose data schemes of balanced search trees are comparison based. This fact explains why these trees are also named comparison trees. They answer ***contains*** and ***range queries*** without metric information. The great degree of generality in conjunction with the high performance makes search trees useful in numerous practical applications, which process large datasets. However, the straightforward use of search trees is not effective in solving such important real-world problems as classification and clustering.

One obvious issue is that a comparison does not tell us how close or distant are two given elements. Thus, we cannot answer if these two elements are related to each other or not in a user problem. The other issue is much more challenging. In most applications, one object has several properties. Its numerical model represents an element associated with several data similar to a point defined by several coordinates. This fact makes the problem of clustering multi-dimensional. A search tree offers only one-dimensional ordering, typically lexicographical. The drawback of such ordering is that mapping from multi-dimensional space does not preserve proximity of elements, because the distance between two elements cannot be computed through a comparison. As a result, nearest elements in such a tree are reshuffled. The distance between two successive elements can become significantly greater than any distance to a nearest neighbor of each element.

Using balanced trees for the analysis of multi-dimensional data is still possible, but it is not as trivial as supporting basic search operations. The method, which significantly improves proximity of mapping from multi-dimensional to one-dimensional space, is based on a space filling curve. A good choice for practical implementations is Morton or Peano-Hilbert curve. The ordering of objects stored in a tree is defined by the space filling curve. The method is both time and space efficient, since the tree provides a wide variety of efficient operations and stores only non-empty grid cells.

The one-dimensional datasets and problems, which are the subject of this book, do not have the proximity complications discussed above. Data analysis methods do not need a space filling method, since any one-dimensional curve optimally fills one-dimensional space. In an ordered one-dimensional dataset, sequential ordering is identical to spatial ordering. Any pair of consecutive elements defines a segment or interval that contains no other element in the middle. In sequential order, a next element is the nearest to its previous element. In reverse sequential order, a previous element is the nearest to its next element. In this book, a data scheme is metric, if a distance between any two elements of a dataset is defined. We use only the Euclidean distance, which is particularly simple in one-dimensional space.

2.9 GEOMETRIC PRESENTATION AND VISUALIZATION OF ALGORITHMS

The effective analysis of a complex problem takes advantage of a variety of tools that deal with different aspects of the problem. The visualization of algorithms on data structures is an important method of this analysis. Its primary aim is to help us better understand the structural relationships between elements of a dataset and the dynamics of algorithms on data structures. With the right choice of a visualization method, details of complex algorithms become more transparent. One good diagram helps us to avoid writing a lengthy explanation. With a wrong choice, the algorithms become more difficult to understand. Finding the optimal visual representation is an iterative process that involves experiments not only with different types of views and visual attributes but also with different levels of mathematical and model abstraction.

The simplicity of one-dimensional problems is both an advantage and an interesting aspect of the design of data structures. It often makes useful geometric presentation of data structures, even if a data type of a user element does not provide a distance function. The geometry based approach helps us visualize and explain efficient algorithms on complex augmented data structures. The graphical presentation and drawing of data structures are important not only for illustrations but also for the design of new algorithms. In this context, comparison based and distance based data scheme have the following specifics.

Drawing of data structures with comparison based data schemes has a great degree of flexibility, since their graphical presentations do not know about distances between keys. In a diagram of a search tree, it is sufficient to show the structural relationships between nodes, such as child-parent. A better presentation of the search tree guarantees the correct ordering of keys. However, such a presentation is not always used in articles and textbooks due to space limitation. For the same reason, the diagrams of data structures in this book may not follow the rules of the most precise presentation.

The data structures with distance based data schemes are rigid. In addition to the connectivity of nodes, a rigid data structure has a shape. Ideally, its diagram must correctly show both ordering of elements and values of distances between consecutive elements. In practice, the last requirement is not easy to meet, since a graphical presentation should be compact to fit into the page drawing area.

One of the main goals of this book is to introduce fast summation algorithms and algorithms that support efficient representation of a sequence. The geometric interpretation is attractive for this purpose because it provides intuitively clear diagrams that help readers understand various aspects of algorithms and data structures. However, the human intuition can be insufficient and even misleading when it comes to implementing algorithms with a limited set of facilities offered by a programming language. Computers do not have the human ability of processing of visual information. The realization of what is obvious for a human in a computer system normally requires an advanced mathematical model and a substantial amount of code.

In order to demonstrate how the design methods work, we need a basic data structure that meets several requirements. Its structure should be relatively simple to take advantage of the geometric interpretation and help us understand the key ideas. The data structure should also provide efficient primary operations for processing of large datasets, such as insertion, deletion and search. These requirements are almost obvious. However, the next one is interesting and might be a bit surprising. It comes from the mathematical definition of summation. The important aspect of the design and implementation of new fast algorithms is that the mathematical rules of summation are formulated for sequences, but not for sets as it might be expected.

Some of the basic data structures that we discussed are not the best choice for this purpose. A linked list has a very simple structure and provides good support for sequences, but it is not acceptable due to poor performance of search and access to distant data elements. On the other hand, a basic balanced tree, such as a red-black tree, offers many efficient primary operations, but its facilities for the representation of sequences are problematic due to non-linear structure. As any hierarchical data structure, a tree provides a partition of a data space into ranges induced by data points stored in its nodes. The difficulty of the visualization using a tree is caused by the fact that end points of partition ranges are located at different levels.

The well-known data structure, which is more suitable for the development and explanation of fast summation algorithms, is a skip list. Its variant with randomized structure is usually described in the context of efficient support for dictionaries. This variant of a skip list offers a number of advantages important for practical applications, including simple implementation of primary operations. The main disadvantage is that the skip list guarantees logarithmic performance of these operations on average only, since randomization does not guarantee that its structure is balanced. These issues are addressed in the deterministic variants of skip lists, but they are not so widely known and discussed in the literature.

At the same time, the structure of skip lists is similar to that of the level linked data structures discussed above. This fact explains our choice of level linked B+-trees for the development of new efficient algorithms (see Figure 2.10). The use of classical data structures minimizes the risk of failure and has numerous benefits. The main one is that these data structures have been thoroughly studied and tested in large scale applications. B+-trees offer simple implementations for a wide variety of primary algorithms, but, unlike randomized skip lists, they guarantee logarithmic performance of these operations in the worst case.

For geometric analysis, a level linked B+-tree has yet another important property. Its structure is globally balanced. Because of this property and linear structure of a list at each level, a diagram of such a tree looks like a set of layers. For illustration purposes, we use a simplified structure of a B+-tree. It has only one link between a parent and its first child. For all other children in the same group, the links are implicit. The parent can be reached by moving to the first child. The minimization of the number of

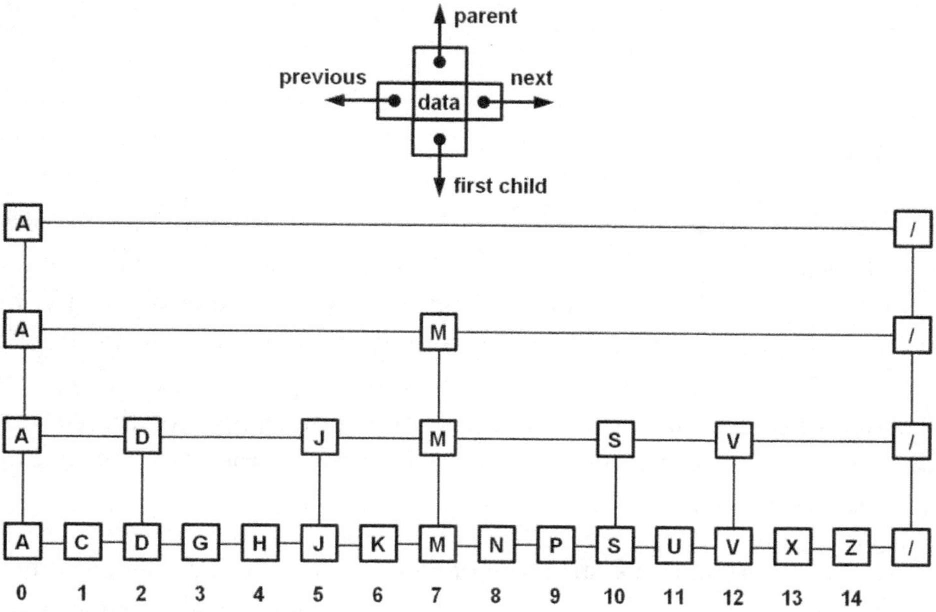

Figure 2.10: Illustration of a level linked variant of a search B+-tree with a small branching factor and a data scheme of a skip list. The linked list of the deepest level stores a given dataset. The internal nodes in vertical chains store multiple copies of keys of the dataset elements.

explicit child-parent links avoids the issues of cumbersome graphical illustrations without loss of key functionality required for the development of fast algorithms. The simplified balanced structure of level linked B+-trees works well for comparison based and distance based data schemes. It is more helpful in the analysis of algorithms than the structure of a randomized skip list. Note that the practical implementations of B+-trees take advantage of more complex connectivity to achieve the best performance of specified operations.

In addition to B+-trees, we use perfect binary trees, which offer compact illustrations for explanation of algorithms. There is no significant difference between these types of trees in the efficient algorithms that we will focus on. These trees, however, are different in terms of their typical practical applications. B+-trees provide a wider variety of efficient operations, whereas the perfect binary trees with rigid structure can take advantage of very fast array representations.

2.10 SUMMARY

In the design and analysis of algorithms, a data structure can be often viewed as a structured storage. The best possible performance of the important operations of insertion and deletion is determined by the structural invariants, which are independent of specific data schemes. The local connectivity of nodes in a data structure is responsible for the efficiency of sequential processing. The maximum length of the shortest path between two arbitrary nodes is the measure of the speed of random access and search.

The ability to combine one structure of connected nodes or cells with more than one data scheme enables us to extend the range of efficient primary operations and, thus, the application area of our data structures. A trivial example of using one structure with two different data schemes is an array that can store either an unordered or an ordered dataset. The advantage of an ordered array is that it offers much more efficient search algorithms. Another example is a binary tree, which provides efficient support either for a binary heap or for a binary search tree with an appropriate choice of a data scheme.

In the real-world applications processing large datasets, the requirements for performance are particularly strict. The running time of an operation is expected to be logarithmic or better in the worst case. A set and a sequence are the main mathematical concepts used in programming solutions. The set operations are well supported by basic data structures, such as balanced search trees, hash tables and in some cases ordered arrays. At the same time, each basic data structure offers limited facilities in terms of the representation of a sequence. The classical sequences (linked lists and arrays) have different performance characteristics. Each of them has advantages and disadvantages. Trees are not natural sequences due to their non-linear structure. They offer reasonable facilities for sequential processing of a whole dataset but are not optimal for range queries. The main practical issue of basic data structures is that one inefficient operation can cause performance degradation even in relatively simple applications.

A B+-tree is a complex data structure that consists of a balanced tree and a linked list. The combination avoids inefficiencies by using the strength of its constituent parts. In terms of the performance of primary operations, two basic data structures complement each other. The improvement in overall performance suggests that not only nodes of the deepest level but also internal nodes of each level can be connected to form a link list. The enhanced level linked connectivity of a B+-tree offers the benefit of a wider set of efficient primary operations. The combination of different types of data structures also offers a greater degree of flexibility in storing a user dataset and various implementation specific data. This is an attractive feature for the development of new efficient algorithms.

The wide variety of data structures and algorithms is crucial to deal with even wider variety of problems that we can solve using programming methods. For large and complex problems, a data structure is only one element of a solution. At early stages of the development of a programming solution, we consider all of the potentially useful data structures. The ease of the implementation is one of the main factors, which determines our choice for the first version of a solution. The basic data structures play an important role in the initial development. The drawback of such solutions is that they may cause serious performance problems that make them unacceptable for processing of large datasets. These issues are normally addressed with advanced data structures at subsequent and final stages of the development.

Chapter 3: Sequences Based on Efficient Counting

Our approach to the description of algorithms and data structures is different from that in textbooks. Instead of classical search algorithms on balanced trees, our main focus is on the efficient representation of a mathematical sequence in programming languages. At first, we introduce a simple variant of an advanced data structure that supports an unordered sequence. Then, we consider a bit more complex ordered sequence, which provides search operations with the performance equal to that of basic balanced trees.

Suppose that we use for processing of datasets a computer system and a programming language, which do not provide built-in arrays. The system supports only data structures of linked nodes, such as lists and search trees. As discussed in Chapter 2, basic variants of these data structures are not always the best choice for applications that require efficient sequences. To avoid performance issues, we need new data structures that support facilities of sequences with the efficiency compatible with that of arrays. The non-trivial problem, which we face, is how to design a linked data structure that can provide a replacement for an array. In this chapter, we will consider methods that allow us to develop a sensible alternative to an array.

We start with algorithms for efficient random access to data elements, since this is the main strength of arrays, which offer constant time operations. We show how to achieve logarithmic running time of random access to data stored in an advanced linked data structure. This performance is a bit worse than that of arrays. However, it represents a significant improvement compared to basic linked lists. In addition, the advanced linked data structures deliver much better performance of insert and erase operations, which are slow on arrays. For this reason, these data structures outperform arrays in large scale applications that require a wide variety of operations.

3.1 WHY WE NEED FAST COUNTING

The title of this chapter tells us that our goal is to develop the representation of a mathematical sequence, which is internally based on a method of efficient counting elements in a dataset. In order to understand why such a method is crucial to the efficient representation of a sequence, we will examine the formal mathematical definition of this concept.

In mathematics, a sequence is defined as a function that maps an element of the set of non-negative integers into an element of a given dataset. In a sequence, elements are numbered for identification purposes. Each element in a sequence has a rank, which represents the total number of elements before this element. The rank is a unique identifier of the element. The rank can be also regarded as an external label assigned to an element by a sequence, since the rank of the element does not depend on the value of the element. A sequence does not place the restriction that its elements be ordered. Unlike a set, a sequence can contain duplicate values. In programming languages, a rank of an element is usually named a subscript, an index or a position in linear order. A group of consecutive elements or a range in a sequence is defined through the ranks of the first and last elements.

Any data structure that provides a method of counting data elements in sequential order meets the mathematical requirements. It is important to note that the performance of counting is not specified in the definition of a mathematical sequence. This freedom is the reason for different interpretations and programming implementations of a sequence. For example, a linked list is a classical sequence, but its random access is too slow for many practical applications. The method of counting elements using links between nodes has linear running time. The search for an element specified by its rank has the same performance. To avoid confusion with arrays, programming implementations of linked lists do not usually offer the subscript operator.

3.2 CONSTRUCTION OF STRUCTURED STORAGE

Before we start an analysis of a user dataset, we must know how to build a data structure that supports required efficient operations and primary algorithms. At this stage, we are interested in storage properties of our data structures. The details of a data scheme are not important yet. As discussed in Chapter 2, the storage facilities are determined by the structural invariants that do not depend on specific data schemes.

In many practical situations, an initial dataset is specified before we start processing. For example, the data are provided by a user. Another typical situation is the conversion from a different type of a data structure. If the dataset is large, we need a fast construction algorithm, which prepares our data structure to store the given number of elements. A level linked B+-tree provides for this purpose the following bottom-up algorithm (see Figure 3.1), which has linear running time.

The first step is the construction of a linked list with the number of nodes equal to the size of a given dataset plus one for the special end node. This is the straightforward algorithm that appends newly created nodes to the end of the list. In each node, the memory region for a data element is allocated, but not yet initialized with a specific value.

The second step is the construction of linked lists of internal levels of the tree. This is iterative processing that builds a new level on top a previous one. In terms of connectivity, each node of internal level has at most four links. Left and right links connect previous and next sibling neighbors of a doubly linked list of a tree level. Two vertical links up and down connect a leftmost child with its parent. These vertical links are responsible for the balance and high performance of primary operations of this structure.

Given the minimum degree of a node t, the number of children in a balanced B+-tree varies between t and $2t$. Since the total number of elements is given, the construction algorithm can build the groups of children of approximately equal size. The size of $1.5t$ is optimal to reduce the frequency of split and merge operations in subsequent processing. The size of $2t$ enables us to build a tree with the minimum height.

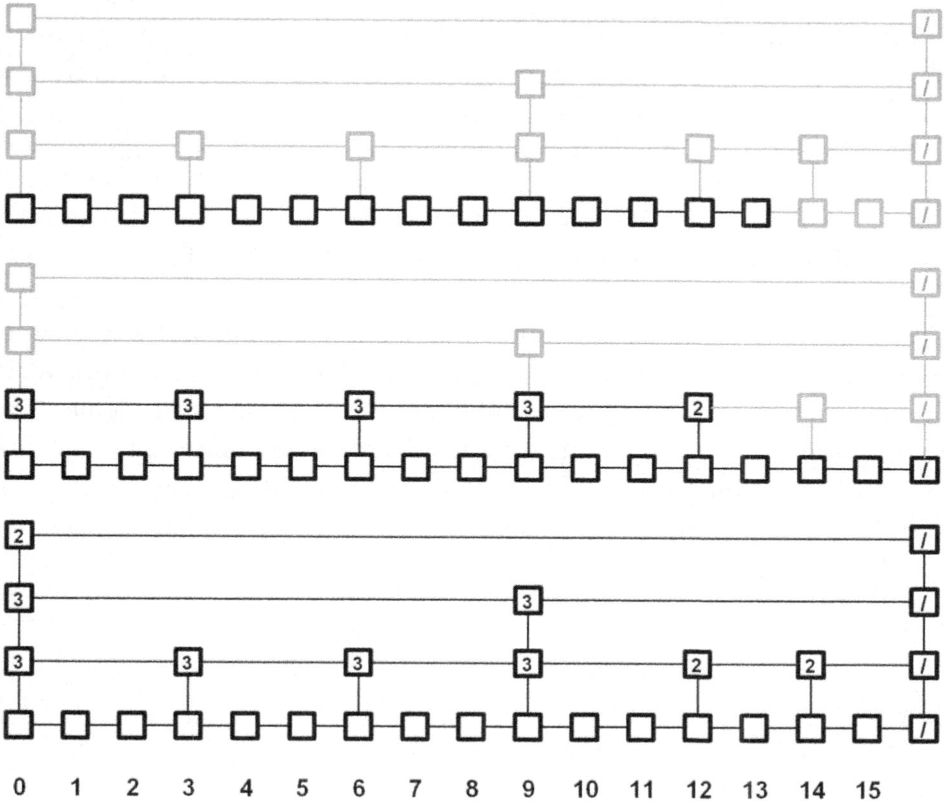

Figure 3.1: Illustration of the bottom-up construction of a level linked B+-tree. Internal nodes store counts of children.

Similarly to the deepest level, a linked list of an internal level is constructed by appending new nodes to the end of the list. The difference is that this algorithm uses the last complete top list to count child nodes. A new parent node and two vertical links are created only when this algorithms finds a valid group of children. The size of each new list constructed drops rapidly, because the average number of children in a B+-tree is large. The iterative processing stops when the number of nodes at the top level becomes less than the maximum size of a group of child nodes. The number of levels and the height of the resulting tree are logarithmic in the number of elements in a given user dataset.

The bottom-up construction of a level linked B+-tree is an example of an algorithm using counts of children. This important structural information is required in all of the internal algorithms that keep the tree balanced. The counts of children are required in operations that split and merge nodes. When a B+-tree has a large branching factor, the counts of children are normally saved in parent nodes in order to improve performance of various primary algorithms by avoiding unnecessary re-counting.

3.3 RANK ALGORITHM USING COUNTS OF CHILDREN

The counts of children saved in parent nodes can be used in the algorithms of sequence facilities too. For example, consider a rank algorithm, which counts elements of a user dataset. Since specific values of data elements are not important at this stage, it is sufficient to consider counting nodes of the deepest level, which provide storage for elements of the user dataset. The complex structure of a level linked B+-tree (see Figure 3.2) supports two algorithms.

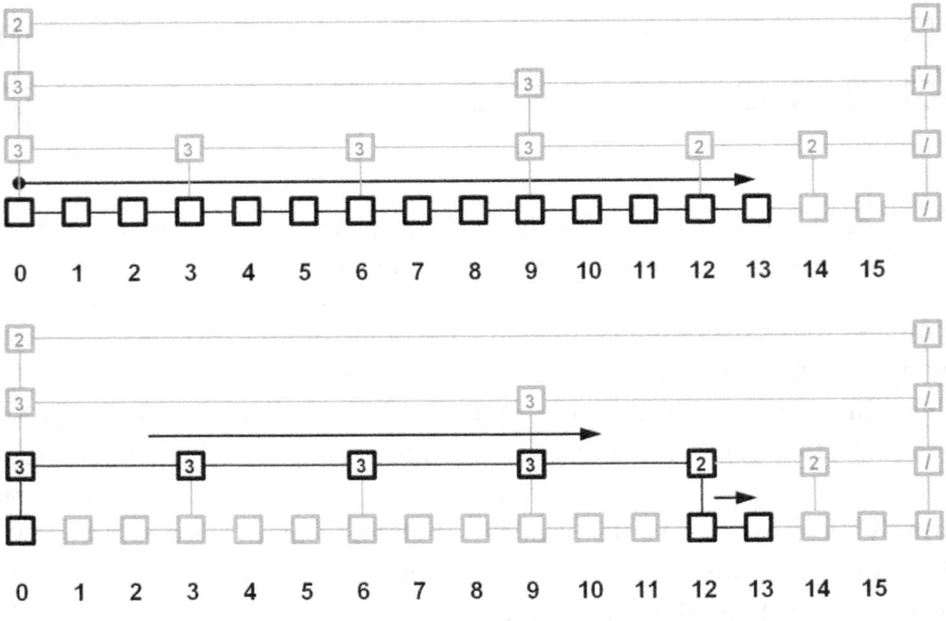

Figure 3.2: Two rank algorithms using two deepest levels. The path through the linked list of the deepest level has 13 links, the path through internal nodes - 7 links.

The standard algorithm on a linked list of the deepest level of the tree visits each node. The faster algorithm is based on the observation that the first internal level is built on top of the deepest list, which is designed to store elements of a user dataset. For nodes of this internal level only, counts of children are identical to counts of nodes with data elements. The faster algorithm starts search for a node specified by a rank from the first node of this internal level. It moves from left to right using horizontal links of the internal level and computes the total number of nodes of the deepest level by summing up counts of children in the visited nodes. The algorithm moves down and visits a small number of nodes of the deepest level only at last stage of the search.

The algorithm of counting sequence elements based on the counts of children has linear running time in the number of visited parent nodes. Compared to straightforward counting elements in a linked list, the number of operations is reduced by the factor equal to the average size of a child group. For a tree with a large branching factor, this performance improvement can be substantial and acceptable for some practical applications. However, this is not a general purpose method, since its asymptotic performance is linear. Our task is to develop the algorithm, which addresses this issue and guarantees logarithmic performance of counting sequence elements in the worst case.

3.4 TOP-DOWN RANK ALGORITHM

Despite the fact that we have not achieved required performance, the rank algorithm using counts of children deserves a more detailed analysis, because it is faster than the standard algorithm. The first obvious advantage of this algorithm is that its search path through parent nodes is shorter than that of the algorithm using the linked list of the deepest level. With this fact, it is not difficult to notice that, if we start the same search from third or fourth internal level, a path to a node of the deepest level can be made even shorter. The general observation is that the higher level, at which we start the search, the shorter the path and the better performance that we expect to achieve. However, the choice of a specific level still has the limitation of the potential performance improvement only by a constant factor against the standard sequential counting algorithm on the deepest level.

The optimal path, which is guaranteed to have logarithmic length in the number of data elements, starts at the first node of the top level of the tree. This property of the level linked structure is similar to the property of a basic balanced tree that the length of a shortest path between the root and any other node does not exceed the height of the tree, see Chapter 2. Thus, at this stage of the analysis it is reasonable to expect achieving logarithmic performance of a new rank algorithm, which uses a shortest path from the top level of a level linked tree.

The second advantage of the faster rank algorithm is that it uses counts of children stored in parent nodes of the tree. This is an important feature of this algorithm, since a shorter path to a node with a given rank by itself does not guarantee the performance improvement that we achieved. Without pre-computed and saved counts of children any algorithm must re-count a required sub-set of nodes in the list of the deepest level. The task of re-counting nodes is quite costly. It takes time linear in the specified rank value. The overall performance of the algorithm visiting nodes of different levels and re-counting nodes in one level can be even worse than that of the sequential algorithm using one level only.

The discussion of the rank algorithm using counts of children in parent nodes reveals two important features that enable us to improve performance of a rank algorithm. The faster algorithm is based on the combination of a shorter path with pre-computed values stored in nodes of a tree. The idea of this approach enables us to complete the design of the data structure that supports the required rank algorithm with logarithmic running time.

One sub-problem we have already solved. In our data structures, the best possible algorithm uses a shortest path, which starts at the first node of the top level. All we have to do now is to combine the shortest path algorithm with the right type of data, which are stored in internal nodes of the tree. For the best performance, these data should help the new rank algorithm to avoid any needless and costly re-computations at any level of a tree. The counts of children do not meet this requirement. They are suitable for parent nodes of the deepest level list only.

In order to equip the new algorithm with the best suitable type of data for internal nodes of a level linked tree, we will have a look at the definition of a mathematical sequence. It suggests that the key method in any representation of a sequence is the rank method. The efficiency of this method is crucial to the overall performance of the representation. The easiest to implement on computer systems is the definition of the rank as the number of elements in sequence before a selected element.

In our level linked data structures, the sequence elements are stored in the nodes of the linked list of the deepest level. In the context of algorithms on these data structures, a count of sequence elements is equivalent to a count of nodes in the deepest list that store these elements. The definition of sequence rank suggests that high performance of implementation algorithms can be achieved with a data type associated with counts of nodes of the deepest level, rather than with counts of children. Since the new efficient rank algorithm can pass through all of the levels of the tree, it is desirable that each internal node had the optimal count of nodes of the deepest list, which completely avoids or minimizes re-computations that have been discussed above.

But what is the optimal count of such nodes to be stored in an internal node? The answer to this question is provided by the structure of a tree. This value can be defined using the fundamental property of a tree that each internal node is the root of a sub-tree. The requirements for the efficient representation of a sequence can be satisfied, if we choose to store in each internal node a count of nodes of the deepest level of a sub-tree rooted at this internal node. Figure 3.3 shows an example of a level linked data structure with such pre-computed counts, which also represent the numbers of consecutive elements in a sequence. For illustration purposes, this figure also shows at the deepest level the count of 1 for each element of the sequence.

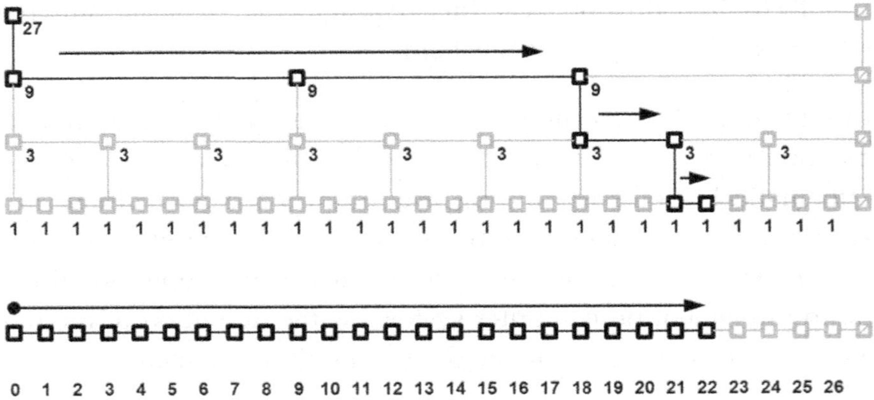

Figure 3.3: A level linked B+-tree with counts of sequence elements. Each internal node stores the number of consecutive elements of a sequence in a sub-tree rooted at the node. The path in black illustrates the top-down search for a node at the deepest level with a given rank. For comparison, this figure also shows the sequential algorithm on a linked list.

Now that we have equipped our level linked tree with required pre-computed data, we can describe the fast rank algorithm, which uses a shortest path from the top level of a level linked tree and efficient counting sequence elements.

The algorithm represents a top-down search for a node at the deepest level that stores a sequence element associated with a specified rank. A typical implementation of this algorithm on a level linked B+-tree uses two variables: a total count of nodes of the deepest level, which is designed to accumulate the number of sequence elements processed by the algorithm, and a pointer to the current node, which provides the search path. The total count is initialized to zero. The pointer points to the start of the search path, which is the first node at the top level. The search is expected to terminate at the deepest level of the tree. The end node of the search path stores the sequence element associated with the specified rank.

For the demo code, we assume that each node of a level linked B+-tree stores the minimal set of links to adjacent nodes and the count of sequence elements:

```
struct Node
{
    // pointer to next node
    NodePointer next;
    // pointer to node one level down
    NodePointer down;
    // size of sub-tree
    int count;
    // sequence value
    int value;
    ...
};
```

Normally, there is no need to store such a count in nodes of the deepest level, since each count at this level has the same value of 1. Similarly, there is no need to store a link to a node one level down, since a node of the deepest level does not have children. These data are redundant. They are not used in practical implementations to save space.

With this simplifying assumption, the search for a node at the deepest level specified by its rank can look like this:

```
// count of sequence elements
int count = 0;
// start search at first node of top level
NodePointer p_node = p_top_start;

do
{
    // traverse linked list of current level
    while ( (count + p_node->count)<=rank )
    {
        // add count
        count = count + p_node->count;
        // move forward
        p_node = p_node->next;
    }

    // move down one level
    p_node = p_node->down;
}
// test if we reached the deepest level
while ( p_node!=0 );

// pointer to node specified by input rank
return p_node;
```

As discussed earlier, the shortest path algorithm by itself does not guarantee the high performance of a rank algorithm. The second factor of achieving high efficiency of the rank algorithm is that the data in visited nodes are designed to support efficient counting. The property that enables us to minimize the number of operations is that the values of counts of sequence elements are significantly larger in nodes of high levels than in nodes of low levels. Thus, the optimal strategy for efficient counting is to visit as many nodes at each level as possible before moving down. As the algorithm moves forward through the linked list of the current level, it adds the counts of sequence elements stored in visited nodes to the total count. At each level, the moves forward are controlled by the condition that the total count is less than or equal to the specified rank. When the last suitable node at the current level is reached, the algorithm moves one level down to continue the search, but the total count does not change. At the deepest level the algorithm moves forward and increments the total count of nodes as in an ordinary linked list, since in each visited node a count is equal to 1. The search terminates when the total count is equal to the specified rank and the algorithm reaches the deepest level. The algorithm may return either a pointer to the last visited node of the deepest level or a reference to the element stored in this node.

The running time of this top-down algorithm is guaranteed to be logarithmic in the number of sequence elements. It is determined by the number of visited levels, which is logarithmic, and the maximum size of a single group of child nodes in a B+-tree, which is constant. This is a substantial improvement over sequential search on a linked list. The length of a search path is also logarithmic. In a tree with a large branching factor, the path has only the small number of parent-child links, which is equal to the number of levels minus one. All of the other links on the path are links that support moves from current to next nodes.

The initialization of counts of sequence elements can be efficiently performed at the construction stage of a B+-tree. As before, we consider the case of a given user dataset. In terms of storage facilities, the algorithm needs to know only the total number of elements, because these counts are structural invariants, which are independent of specific values of elements.

The algorithm of bottom-up construction of a level linked B+-tree, which stores in internal nodes counts of sequence elements, is very similar to the algorithm that initializes counts of children. The main difference is in the method of computing counts of sequence elements. The value of a count in a parent node is equal to the sum of similar counts in child nodes. Unlike counts of children, counts of sequence elements are not reset at each new level. They are accumulated from the whole sub-tree. Their values grow quickly as the construction algorithm moves up.

Because of the close similarity, the performance of these two construction algorithms is basically the same. Note also that in advanced variants of level linked B+-trees one internal node stores counts of both children and sequence elements. In this case, the bottom-up construction algorithm computes two types of counts simultaneously.

3.5 COMPARISON OF TWO RANK ALGORITHMS

The two fast rank algorithms discussed so far are similar in terms of using counts stored in internal nodes. However, they have different efficiency. Compared to the rank algorithm based on counts of children (see Figure 3.2), the top-down rank algorithm (see Figure 3.3) delivers significantly better performance, since its optimal search path starts at the top level of a tree instead of the lowest internal level. This algorithm has logarithmic performance because it uses all of the levels of a tree, whereas the other algorithm uses only two lowest levels. In terms of the effectiveness of using the structure of a level linked B+-tree, the algorithm based on counts of children can be regarded as a simplified variant of the top-down algorithm. Alternatively, the top-down algorithm can be regarded as an improved and advanced variant of the algorithm using counts of children.

The benefit of storing counts of sequence elements is similar to that of storing counts of children. Both types of counts save running time by avoiding re-counting proper nodes in a level linked tree. Nevertheless, in terms of performance of primary algorithms, there is an important difference between counts of children and counts of sequence elements.

A balanced tree has an upper bound on a count of children. Because of this constraint, re-counting children of one group is a constant time operation. Saving counts of children is a good option for large branching factor, but it increases space requirement and has an effect on performance. When branching factor is small, it might be more efficient to simply re-count children and avoid storing the counts. In any case, the running times of the operations, which use counts of children, asymptotically remains the same. For these reasons, storing counts of children in internal nodes of a tree is optional. It is a matter of performance fine tuning at last development stages.

Unlike a count of children, there is no upper bound on a count of sequence elements. Its value can be as large as the size of the whole dataset. Re-counting elements at the deepest level cannot be regarded as a constant time operation. It has linear running time, which is too costly for large datasets. This is why, saving and storing counts of sequence elements in internal nodes of a level linked tree is vital to achieving significant performance gain in operations that use this type of counts.

In order to better understand the difference between two types of counts, consider another interesting property of a level linked B+-tree that stores counts of sequence elements. Since each internal node of the tree represents the root of a sub-tree, the set of nodes at each internal level partitions the set of nodes with consecutive sequence elements at the deepest level. The higher internal level, the coarser is the granularity of such a partition. In addition to this, the partition becomes more and more unbalanced. This is why, the balance of the partition of the deepest level is not guaranteed in the worst case. This is a significant difference from the local partition of nodes into groups of children, which is balanced at each level.

Since the size of a child group is not significant for achieving logarithmic performance of the rank algorithm, in further diagrams we do not normally show the counts of children.

3.6 FINGER SEARCH ALGORITHM

The important advantage of the level linked B+-trees over basic balanced trees is the rich connectivity of nodes. The fast top-down rank algorithm is not the only algorithm useful for efficient representation of a sequence. The combination of tree and list connectivity in one data structure provides another interesting algorithm, which is called finger search. The theoretically attractive feature of this algorithm is that its running time is logarithmic in the number of elements in a given range instead of the total number of elements in a tree. The algorithm is faster because the set of level links enables efficient local search, which avoids visiting the root of a tree. The classical balanced search trees, such as a red-black tree, offer efficient top-down search, but these trees do not support finger search.

The finger search algorithm starts and terminates at two nodes of the deepest level of a level linked tree. The start node and its rank are provided by a client algorithm. The task of finger search is to find the terminal node, which is specified by the rank only. Obviously, the algorithm should be different from sequential search on the linked list of the deepest list, which takes linear running time.

A level linked B+-tree has the interesting property that helps us break the linear running time barrier. A path between two distant nodes of the deepest level is shorter through internal nodes than through nodes of the deepest level (see Figure 3.4). Since there are many paths connecting two nodes of the deepest level, our main interest is in the optimal path that minimizes the number of computational steps and the running time of the algorithm.

Because finger search starts and terminates at the deepest level, the algorithm has two stages of search: bottom-up and top-down. The algorithm for the second stage has been already developed. We can use for finger search the fast top-down rank algorithm, which has the required logarithmic performance. Our task is now reduced to the development of an efficient bottom-up algorithm for the first stage of finger search. To achieve the best performance, the length of this search path should be minimal. The end node of the path represents the root of a sub-tree, which is an input parameter for the fast top-down search.

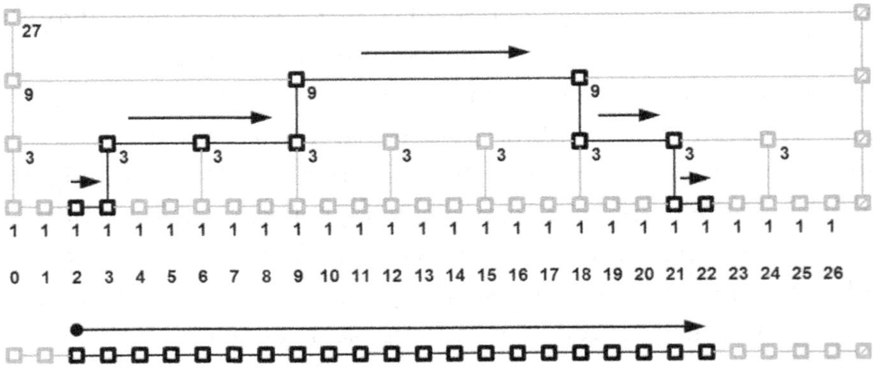

Figure 3.4: Illustration of a shortest path between two nodes of the deepest level. For comparison, this figure shows sequential traversal of a linked list.

The optimal strategy for the bottom-up search is to visit as few nodes at low levels as possible and move up as quickly as possible in order to reach internal nodes with large values of counts of sequence elements. This is why, if a node on the search path has a parent the algorithm moves up, otherwise it moves forward to find the nearest node with a link to parent. To better understand why this strategy is optimal for the performance of the bottom-up search consider the special case when the algorithm starts at the first node of the deepest level. At each level the first node of this data structure has a link to its parent. The chain of such links has the length, which is equal to the number of levels minus one. In a B+-tree with a large branching factor, the chain is significantly shorter than a chain of nodes at the same level that does not have a link to move one level up. However, the total number of such "fast" chains in a level linked B+-tree is relatively small. In the worst case, the performance of bottom-up search is the same as that of top-down search.

Many implementation details of the bottom-up search are similar to those of the top-down search discussed above. The difference is in the condition that terminates the search. The bottom-up algorithm using the optimal strategy moves and counts elements until it finds the node at which the total count is less than or equal to the difference between given ranks of finger search nodes. If the node that we found is at the deepest level, the search terminates. If the node found is internal, finger search starts at this node the top-down rank algorithm to find the terminal node at the deepest level.

The similarity of top-down and finger search algorithms is quite significant (see Figure 3.3 and Figure 3.4). Each algorithm is optimal when it finds a shortest path (not necessary unique) from the first node to the last node. The difference between these algorithms is in the choice of the first node. The top-down algorithm starts at the first node of the top level, whereas the finger search algorithm starts at the node of the deepest level associated with the rank of the first given element of a sequence. For both algorithms, a search path terminates at the node of the deepest level that corresponds to the rank of either a single given element or the second given element.

In theory, finger search is faster than top-down search, because it guarantees logarithmic performance in the distance between positions of two given elements against the total number of elements in a sequence. However, in practical applications, this algorithm does not always outperform the top-down rank algorithm. The obvious drawback for large branching factors and small number of levels is that finger search starts at the deepest level and continues at low levels where counts are small. The bottom-up search can make a significant contribution to the total running time. The same number of operations at the top and high levels is much more effective and quickly narrows the search range. As the distance between two elements of a sequence increases and finger search reaches higher levels, it becomes less efficient than the top-down algorithm. The reality is that the maintenance of two similar algorithms and the need for system specific performance optimization are serious complicating factors for using finger search in the efficient representation of a sequence.

Despite the fact that the top-down rank algorithm is sufficient for most practical implementations of a sequence, the finger search algorithm is superior in such an important application area as fast sequential summation. We will return to algorithms using finger search in Chapter 4 and Chapter 5.

3.7 STORAGE FACILITIES AND AUGMENTING

The storage facilities of a level linked B+-tree are much more advanced than those of basic data structures. Because a B+-tree is a complex data structure, which represents a combination of a B-tree and a linked list, it offers two types of storages. The enhanced storage facilities enable efficient extension of the functionality of these advanced data structures, which is not achievable in basic data structures.

From a user's point of view, the storage facilities of a level linked B+-tree are equivalent those of a linked list, since all of the elements of a user dataset are stored in the nodes of the deepest level (see Figure 3.5). A node of this list stores the minimal set of data: an element and links to adjacent nodes. Compared to a node in a basic linked list, a node of the deepest level has one additional link to a parent.

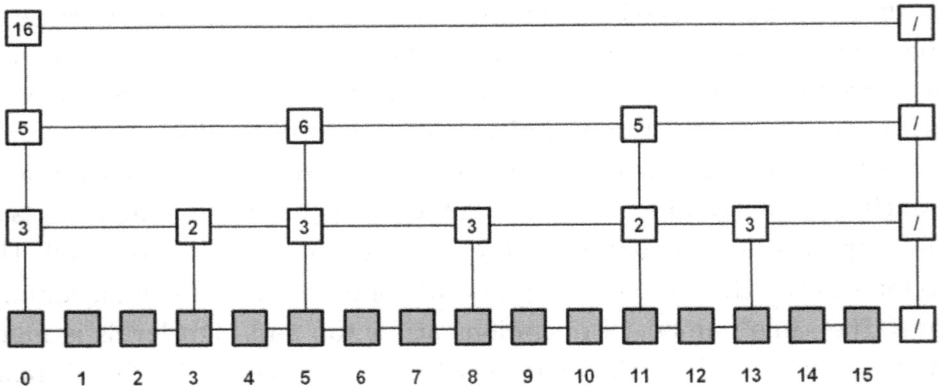

Figure 3.5: A level linked B+-tree that provides space for elements of a user dataset in nodes of the linked list of the deepest level (nodes in gray). The storage places no restriction that the dataset is ordered or contains unique elements only. The internal nodes store counts of consecutive nodes of the deepest level and thus counts of sequence elements.

The strength of B+-trees is in their capability to store not only elements of a given sequence, but also representation specific data. We have already discussed two rank algorithms that benefit from storing counts in internal nodes of a level linked B+-tree. The algorithm using counts of children delivers a constant factor improvement of the performance compared to sequential counting nodes of the deepest level. Although useful in practice, this is not a significant improvement from a theoretical perspective. The algorithm using counts of sequence elements improves the performance from linear to logarithmic. In terms of processing large datasets, this is a breakthrough both in theory and in practice.

This fast rank algorithm is our first example of applying the method of augmenting a data structure. In principle, the method is quite simple. To avoid costly re-computations, it uses a data structure to store data frequently used in client algorithms. This powerful design method represents a variant of the general optimization method, which finds the best balance between time and space efficiency. The considerable performance improvement achieved in the rank algorithm using counts of sequence elements suggests that the method of augmenting data structures has significant potential. This is one of the main design methods that we will use to develop efficient algorithms later in this book.

The space efficiency of the internal special-purpose storage is another important feature of B+-trees. For approximate estimates, the number of internal nodes can be easily computed as the size of a user dataset divided by the minimum degree of a B-tree. In typical in-memory variants of B+-trees, the value of the minimum degree varies between 10 and 100. The relatively small number of internal nodes and the relatively small space required to store these nodes are the essential features of B+-trees that make them highly space efficient and ideal for developing new fast algorithms. To achieve this, we add implementation data, which are associated with a user dataset, to internal nodes only. The extended functionality comes at the cost of only a fractional increase in the space requirement. In contrast, a basic balanced tree offers the homogeneous storage. Each node stores both a user element and implementation data. Any extension of the functionality requires the space, which is proportional to the size of a user dataset.

Since the extension of the functionality and application area comes at the cost of the increased space requirement, it is reasonable to expect that in practical applications time efficiency of previously developed algorithms can be affected too. After augmenting, the performance of algorithms that do not use new implementation data may become a bit worse. The addition of one integer value to all of the internal nodes may increase the running time of such an algorithm by about 10 percent. This relatively small effect on the performance of B+-trees is caused by worsening locality of reference to data. The mathematical analysis ignores such effects. The computational complexities of algorithms that do not use new implementation specific data remain unchanged.

3.8 ITERATOR AND SUBSCRIPT OPERATOR

The object-oriented programming languages offer at least two methods of accessing elements in a sequence through the subscript operator and the iterator. For example, in C++ the following two lines produce the same result:

```
value = sequence[index];
value = *iterator;
```

Although these two methods of using a sequence look similar in the user code, they may have important internal differences. In this section, we discuss why an iterator is the preferable choice to work with advanced data structures.

The concept of an iterator is considered in detail in books on object-oriented programming. It provides a unified interface, which allows a user algorithm to access and process data elements without exposing internals of an underlying data structure. In programming solutions using sequences, an iterator object is an effective alternative to the subscript operator. In accordance with the definition of a mathematical sequence, an iterator represents the position in a sequence and provides a mapping method to access an element at this position. In this respect, if a data structure provides an iterator, it represents a sequence. The specific shapes of iterator facilities vary widely. However, the interface of each iterator includes two types of member functions or operators. The facilities of the first type enable a user algorithm to control the position of an iterator in a sequence. The facilities of the second type allow us to read and modify the value of the element pointed to by the iterator.

The generalization capacity of iterators is based on their facilities, which support a mathematical sequence. The design of containers and algorithms in the C++ standard library is an excellent example of using iterators to achieve a high level of generality and efficiency. In this library, iterators are mediators between underlying data structures of standard containers and algorithms. The containers provide iterators with the uniform interfaces, and the standard algorithms operate through these iterators on data, which are stored in different types of data structures.

The practical challenge for the design of iterators is how to address the issue of significant difference in the performance of sequential and random access to data stored in different types of data structures. The C++ standard library introduces several categories of iterators for basic data structures, such as linked lists and arrays. The pattern can be applied to the library extensions based on advanced data structures. The benefit of using a wide variety of library algorithms is quite significant to ignore in practice.

The augmented level linked B+-trees provide efficient support for both the subscript operator and the random access iterator. However, performance properties of advanced data structures are different from those of basic data structures. For example, consider the following sample code in C++:

```
// reading values through
// the subscript operator
int N = sequence.size();
for (int i=0; i<N; ++i)
    sum += sequence[i];

// reading values through
// an iterator
iterator start = sequence.begin();
iterator end = sequence.end();
for (iterator it=start; it!=end; ++it)
    sum += *it;
```

For an array-based sequence, the running time of both variants of summation is linear. For a sequence using an augmented B+-tree, the situation is less trivial. Access to a sequence element through the subscript operator has computational cost $O(\log N)$ in the worst case. Thus, the total cost of sequential reading all the values through the subscript operator is $O(N \log N)$. In order to achieve linear performance of reading consecutive elements in a sequence, a user algorithm should use sequential access through an iterator, such as shown in the second variant. Obviously, it is not only interesting but also important to understand such a difference in the performance of similar variants of using the same data structure.

The advantages of iterator-based solutions follow from the fact that iterators are objects. An iterator has a state that includes its current position in a sequence. In addition, an iterator has access to internal algorithms and data of the state of the data structure, which the iterator refers to. For these reasons, an iterator has the ability to choose the optimal algorithm to move to a new position. The decision depends on the distance between the current and new positions and the size of a sequence.

In order to move to a next or previous element, the iterator uses links to adjacent nodes in the list of the deepest level. The computational cost of increment and decrement operators is constant. Thus, the total cost of sequential access to each element through an iterator is linear. Similarly, for a small distance between two positions, the iterator moves through the nodes of the deepest level. Only when the distance becomes large, the iterator switches to the top-down rank algorithm, which has logarithmic performance in the worst case.

The running time of the first variant of summation is worse and cannot be improved, since a user algorithm cannot pass its current position in a sequence. It passes only a new position. With such limited input information, the subscript operator can apply only the top-down rank algorithm to find the element associated with a given rank. Even if the new position is very close to the current one, the search starts from the first node of the top level of a B+-tree.

In C++, an iterator is introduced as a generalization of an ordinary pointer. For this reason, interfaces of iterators mirror ordinary pointers. This design choice helps programmers increase readability of the code. The widest set of operators for pointer arithmetic is provided by random access iterator.

```
iterator position = sequence.begin();
double value = 0.0;

position += 25;
value = *position;
```

The implementation aspect of iterators for basic data structures is almost trivial. Since the original idea behind C++ iterators is to generalize a pointer, these iterators are normally pointer-based. This implementation approach is, however, not quite effective for complex data structures, such as augmented B+-trees. The main complication is that pointers to nodes in a dynamically allocated data structure do not support efficient pointer arithmetic.

It is interesting that a better approach follows directly from the definition of a mathematical sequence. In this variant of an iterator, the main data member is an integer, which represents the rank of an element pointed to by the iterator. In addition, this iterator provides mapping of non-negative integer values into container elements through pointers to nodes of the deepest level. Compared to the subscript operator, which implements the traditional mathematical mapping of integers into sequence elements, the integer-based iterator can be regarded as "inside out" variant of the same mapping. Such an integer-based iterator is both simple and efficient.

3.9 INSERTION AND DELETION

The properties and primary algorithms of B- and B+-trees have been extensively studied for systems with external memory. Their insertion and deletion algorithms are described in detail in the literature and textbooks. The algorithms have logarithmic running time in the worst case. The high performance of the modifying operations is one of the key strengths of these trees.

The main difficulty for insert operation on these trees with large branching factors is overflow of a contiguous block of data. The simplest insertion algorithm is based on the top-down search. It splits each full node on the way down the search path in order to maintain balance and prepare space for a new element. However, our interest is in bottom-up algorithms for the reasons that will become clear below. The bottom-up insertion into these trees is also possible, but it is more complicated. It is implemented through temporary overflow of nodes, which are split when the algorithm moves up.

In-memory B+-trees have much greater degree of flexibility to deal with the problem of node overflow (see Figure 3.6). Unlike on-disk trees, they have almost unrestricted access to system resources and can allocate small or large amount of memory each time when the need arises. The linear connectivity of nodes makes the primary operations on level linked B+-trees almost as simple as those on ordinary linked lists. The other essential

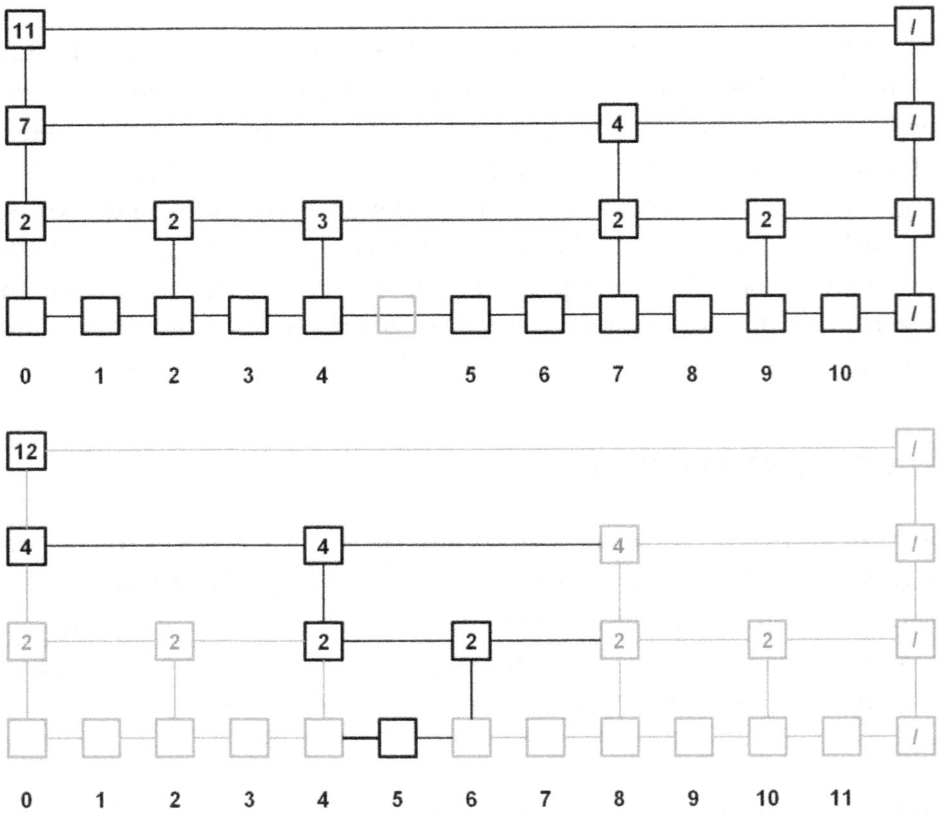

Figure 3.6: Illustration of the insertion of a new node after the fourth node in the deepest list of a tree that has 11 elements of a sequence. The resulting tree with 12 elements shows in black new nodes, new links and nodes with modified values of counts of sequence elements.

feature is the introduction of vertical links that connect parent nodes with appropriate first (or leftmost) child nodes. This set of links provides efficient support for vertical traversal and for the bottom-up algorithms that we are interested in.

The worst case performance of the bottom-up insert operation is due to the fact that inserting one element can cause overflow and splitting nodes at all of the levels of a B+-tree. The split operations produce the most significant changes in the structure. The algorithm of splitting a node in a level linked B+- tree has the simple implementation of adding a new parent node in order to balance children whose size increased. After the insertion of a new node, the algorithm tests the size of the modified group of child nodes against the maximum limit of node overflow. If the size does not exceed the limit the algorithm terminates, otherwise the algorithm splits the modified children into two equal size groups, as follows: It selects from the linked children the middle node, which becomes the first child of the new group of nodes. In order to keep the structure balanced, the algorithm creates a new parent node and inserts it into the list, which is at one level up, after the parent of the original linked children. The last step is to connect the new parent with the first child of the new group. This connection adds a new vertical link to the level linked structure of a B+-tree. Since the new parent node is a child of another parent, the insertion algorithm moves one level up to continue processing of the modified children. Splitting the top level increases the height of the tree.

The bottom-up implementation of the delete operation in some aspects is similar to that of the insert operation. But because the deletion effect is opposite to that of the insertion, the implementation is based on primary algorithms that undo structural changes caused by inserting a new element. The most difficult is the case when the deletion of a node makes the size of children less than the minimum limit of node underflow. One of the options to address this issue is the redistribution of nodes between adjacent siblings at the same level. The option is useful, because it delays the execution of more costly primary algorithm, which restores balance by merging adjacent siblings. In a level linked B+-tree, the merge operation removes a parent and its vertical link to the first child. In the worst case, the delete operation decreases the height of a B+-tree.

The bottom-up operations, which insert or delete a single element, have important practical advantages in terms of performance. These operations take logarithmic time in the worst case only. In the best case, their running time is constant. The explanation of this fact is that these modifying operations are applied directly to user data stored in the linked list of the deepest level of a B+-tree. A group of child nodes represents a smaller linked list, for which insert and delete are constant time operations. On average, adding or removing one element at the deepest level does not immediately violates structural invariants of a B+-tree, since the valid number of children has the range from t to $2t$, where t is the minimum degree of a node.

This feature of B+-trees enables the performance optimization for specific practical applications. We can improve the total running time of a user algorithm by increasing the probability of the constant time operations. This can be easily achieved by adjusting branching factor of a B+-tree. As the branching factor increases, so does the probability of the constant time operations. The insertions or deletions that take logarithmic time become rare events, when the branching factor is large.

In order to take advantage of these high performance bottom-up operations a user is required to provide the position in a sequence. Using for this purpose the rank of an element is not optimal approach, since this variant involves the top-down search to find a node at the deepest level to start a modifying operation. A better option of providing the position for insert and delete operations is to use an iterator, which contains adequate data associated with a B+-tree. This approach avoids the unnecessary top-down search and, thus, saves time logarithmic in the size of a user dataset for each modifying operation.

The high performance of the bottom-up operations allows for efficient processing of large datasets. For example, the incremental construction of a level linked B+-tree, which iteratively inserts single elements, can be faster than the bottom-up construction algorithm described at the beginning of this chapter. Similarly, when we need to empty a tree or remove a large number of consecutive elements the delete operation provides performance that eliminates the need for the development of specialized algorithms. Usually, in processing that involves a large number of consecutive elements of a sequence or a set, the fastest are operations that append a new element or remove the last element.

The method of augmenting provides substantial performance improvement, but it comes at the cost of extra complexity of data structures and implementation of primary algorithms. The insert and delete operations in augmented data structures maintain not only invariants of the structure and basic data scheme but also additional internal data associated with a user dataset. As usual, our ultimate goal in the development of advanced data structures is the highest performance of a user algorithm.

The bottom-up variants of algorithms are the best choice to meet these requirements. First of all, any change in a level linked B+-tree starts in a user dataset, which is stored at the deepest level. The subsequent operations deliver the effect of this change to the nodes at the higher levels of the tree. Another reason is that algorithms for insert and delete operations can achieve high performance in just one bottom-up pass that makes changes to both the underlying tree and additional internal data. The performance of such single pass algorithms is very close to that of algorithms on underlying data structures that have not been augmented. However, because of the added complexity developing such optimal algorithms might be a challenging task. In order to address this complexity issue, it makes sense to start with relatively simple variants, which are based on two or more bottom-up passes.

The first pass applies the primary algorithm of the basic data structure. Its completion guarantees that all of the invariants of the underlying data structure are valid. It also returns new and processed nodes that may store invalid internal data associated with a user dataset. This special subset of nodes is produced by the split, merge and balance operations on the way up a tree. Its size is proportional the height of the tree in the worst case. The second bottom-up pass updates or re-computes for the given subset of nodes additional data only. The loss of performance associated with the second pass is not significant, since all of the update operations on the subset of nodes take time proportional to the height of a tree. The total running time of insert and delete operations remains logarithmic in the size of a user dataset.

The important practical advantage of the two pass variants of insert and delete operations is that they are based on proven algorithms for basic B-

and B+-trees. They are robust, efficient and have been widely used in large scale systems. These algorithms can be re-used in the future for the development of new variants of augmented trees.

3.10 UNORDERED SEQUENCE

We begin with the general purpose representation of an unordered sequence, since it is simpler than the representation of an ordered sequence, which will be discussed later.

The main requirement for this representation follows from the formal definition of a mathematical sequence, refer to Section 3.1. A data structure, which stores a user dataset, is expected to provide access to any element associated with a given rank. The augmented level linked B+-tree (see Figure 3.5) meets this requirement for a sequence, since it supports the efficient rank method based on top-down search and counting data elements (see Figure 3.3).

The representation also supports high performance insert and delete operations, which are important in practical applications that process large datasets. The following table shows computational complexities of the primary operations of this representation. For comparison, it includes two representations based on classical data structures.

	Linked List	Array	Augmented B+-Tree
Insertion	$O(1)$	$O(N)$	$O(\log N)$
Deletion	$O(1)$	$O(N)$	$O(\log N)$
Rank	$O(R)$	$O(1)$	$O(\log N)$

Table 3.1: The computational complexities of primary operations of unordered sequences based on basic data structures and an augmented B+-tree. N is the number of elements in a given dataset. Rank - retrieve an element at a given rank R.

We have already considered several aspects of using these operations and supporting algorithms to achieve the optimal performance of this representation in user algorithms. In this section, we summarize properties of augmented level linked B+-trees with the main focus on their sequence facilities and comparison against arrays. Understanding these aspects is helpful in developing efficient solutions to complex problems.

The augmented level linked B+-tree consists of two data structures: a linked list plus a B-tree. In terms of performance characteristics, these basic data structures complement each other. The combination of simple and complex connectivity gives each data structure the ability to address efficiency issues of another data structure. This feature explains why this variant of a B+-tree supports a wide range of efficient algorithms and sequence facilities not possible with one basic data structure.

In this book, we assume that the general purpose representation of a sequence uses at the deepest level a doubly linked list. This choice guarantees sequential processing of data with equal efficiency in both forward and reverse order. However, the specialized representation of a sequence based on a singly linked list at the deepest level is also useful in some applications. It offers improved space efficiency by the cost of less efficient reverse sequential processing. Instead of linear, it has linearithmic ($N \log N$) performance, since access to a previous element is provided though the top-down rank algorithm. For comparison, a basic singly linked list does not support reverse sequential processing at all.

From a user perspective, which ignores internal complexity of the structure, the augmented B+-tree can be considered as a linked list that has improved performance compared to its basic variant. The crucial implementation detail is how to address performance issues of the basic linked list using a search B-tree that offers a wide variety of efficient operations, which however do not directly support the required representation of a sequence. It is not surprising that insert and delete operations on a search B-tree can be slightly modified to suit the representation. Their logarithmic performance is a bit worse than constant time in linked lists, but it is sufficient for large scale applications.

The least obvious feature of the solution is the combination of search algorithms and counting sequence elements, which delivers the performance of random access close to that in arrays. The primary algorithms of this solution operate on the counts of elements that are stored in internal nodes of the B+-tree. The values of counts do not depend on the values of elements in a sequence. These counts of elements are invariants of the structure, but not a user dataset. For this reason, the internal nodes that store these counts can be regarded as a special sub-structure of the augmented B+-tree. The sub-structure of counts with the fast method of counting elements supports access to any element specified by its rank and, thus, it is the key component that enables the augmented B+ tree to efficiently represent a mathematical sequence. This sub-structure implements the mechanics for the subscript operator, which comes without any effort with arrays. Because of this importance, the sub-structure of counts is supported by each variant of an augmented B+ tree that represents an efficient sequence.

In the context of access to data, our main question is whether this general purpose representation of a sequence has the performance that allows us to replace an array in practical applications. The representation of a sequence takes full advantage of both data structures that constitute a B+-tree. A doubly linked list of the deepest level provides optimal constant time access to previous and next elements of a sequence. The fast top-down rank algorithm, which searches on a B-tree, enables a user to reach distant elements.

The logarithmic performance of this algorithm is not much worse than that of array, but it is substantially better than linear performance of any basic linked data structure, such as a list or a balanced tree. As a result, an augmented level linked B+-tree provides efficient sequential and random access to data elements, which makes it the most reasonable alternative to an array in complex user algorithms. For convenience of replacing an array, the representation based on a B+-tree supports the subscript operator or an iterator, refer to Section 3.8.

When a user algorithm needs storage for its data, an augmented level linked B+-tree offers both basic and advanced facilities. On one hand, these facilities of an augmented level linked B+-tree are as simple as those of a linked list at the deepest level. The nodes of this list provide memory space to store elements of a user dataset. On the other hand, the facilities are much more advanced than in an array, because the internal storage of the

B-tree provides the high degree of freedom in the choice of additional data to implement new fast algorithms. The extension of the efficient functionality does not incur significant space overhead compared to the underlying tree. We will exploit this advanced facility of augmented B+-tree in the next chapters.

Since the deepest level of the augmented B+-tree is a linked list, there is no theoretical restriction on the data scheme for this data structure. Any sequence based on a linear data structure can store both unordered and ordered datasets with multiple or unique elements. As we know, the use of a linked list to store an ordered dataset is sub-optimal due to slow linear time access to distant elements in the list. It is not impossible to apply to linked lists algorithms designed for arrays, but this is not a good idea. The algorithms, such as binary search or quicksort, assume constant time access to data elements. On linked lists they will cause performance bottlenecks.

Unlike a basic linked list, the augmented tree (see Figures 3.3 and 3.4) provides much more efficient random access to data. For this reason, there is the interesting aspect of this sequence representation. The general purpose unordered sequence based on this variant of a level linked B+-tree can store an ordered dataset and, thus, the same tree provides the representation for an ordered sequence too. The array algorithms, which make no sense for basic linked lists, provide respectable and often acceptable performance in practical applications due to logarithmic performance of random access operations on this tree. In particular, the running time of binary search on the augmented level linked B+-tree is proportional to $O(\log^2 N)$. This performance is significantly better than linear performance of sequential search on any data structure. It is also close to the running time of binary search on an array, which is $O(\log N)$.

Obviously, with this kind of algorithms, the tree cannot outperform an array that offers the best possible constant-time random access. To improve efficiency, we need a different approach, which is based on the strength of search trees. This idea helps us to find the problem and suggests the solution.

The general purpose representation of an unordered sequence supports efficient rank algorithm, which uses search operations on counts of the augmented B+-tree. At the same time, this tree does not take advantage of efficient search operations on keys. This means that there is significant potential for performance improvements. For this reason, we will now discuss how to develop the specialized representation of an ordered sequence, which provides the optimal performance of search operations.

3.11 ORDERED SEQUENCE

This section describes the most important aspects of ordered sequences. They are not in the main focus of this book, because they are well covered in textbook chapters on augmented red-black and binary search trees. What we discuss here is just another variant of an improved search tree, which is based on a B+-tree. All of these types of search trees are important in practical applications to implement a set or dictionary.

The augmented level linked B+-tree for an unordered sequence, which we considered above, provides a wide range of efficient primary operations. It almost the right data structure, since it can store not only unordered but also ordered datasets. The only issue of this B+-tree is that it does not support efficient search for a key. The linear running time of a sequential search on a linked list of the deepest level is totally unacceptable for processing large datasets. Binary search is a better choice, but its performance is not good enough compared to balanced search trees. If we address this performance issue, we can obtain the efficient representation of an ordered sequence. Here, we achieve this goal using the method of augmenting.

So far, we have considered variants of augmented level linked B+-trees, which store in internal nodes counts of children and sequence elements. Both of these data types are associated with the structural invariants of a tree. A B+-tree, which supports the required efficient ordered sequence, can be regarded as an augmented variant of a B+-tree for an unordered sequence (see Figure 3.7). The distinctive feature of the new B+-tree is that its internal nodes store an additional dataset of keys associated with elements of a user dataset. The deepest level of the new tree remains unchanged, since a linked list can store both ordered and unordered data.

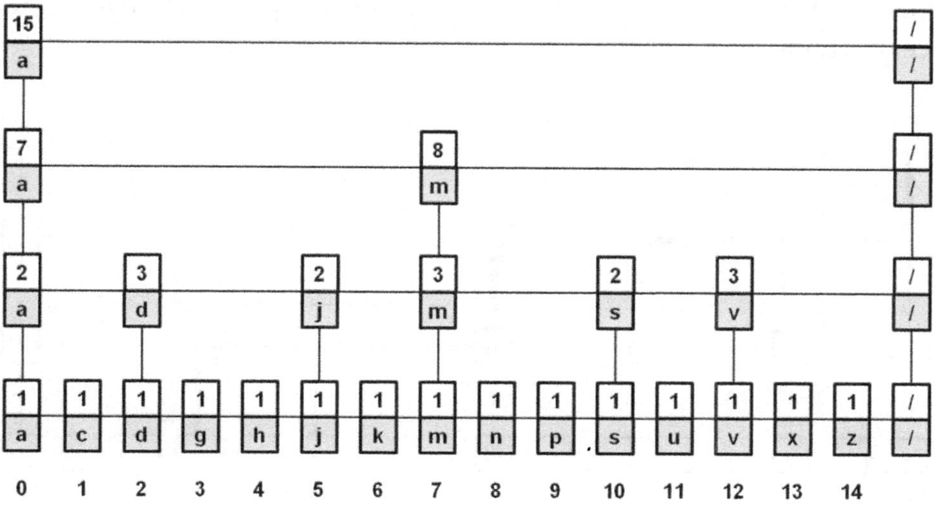

Figure 3.7: An augmented level linked B+-tree that supports an efficient ordered sequence. The internal nodes of the tree store both counts of sequence elements and keys. The counts of 1 in the nodes of the deepest level have been added for illustration purposes only.

This variant of the efficient ordered sequence implements a combination of two datasets in one data structure. The designs of this B+-tree takes advantage of the fact that a structural storage is independent of a data scheme. Compared to the representation of an unordered sequence, the ordered variant requires more space. However, the increase in the space is relatively small, since the new data of keys are added to internal nodes only. Storing two implementation datasets is almost as efficient as storing one implementation dataset. This space efficiency is one of the significant practical advantages of B+-trees.

The new dataset in internal nodes is designed to support efficient search operations on keys. In order to better understand how it works, let us remove counts of sequence elements from the augmented tree (see Figure 3.8). The data structure that we obtained represents a basic level linked B+-tree with the data scheme of skip lists. It belongs to the group of balanced search trees, which guarantee logarithmic running time of search, insertion and deletion. These basic data structures also support efficient sequential access, but they are slow in applications that require frequent random access to data.

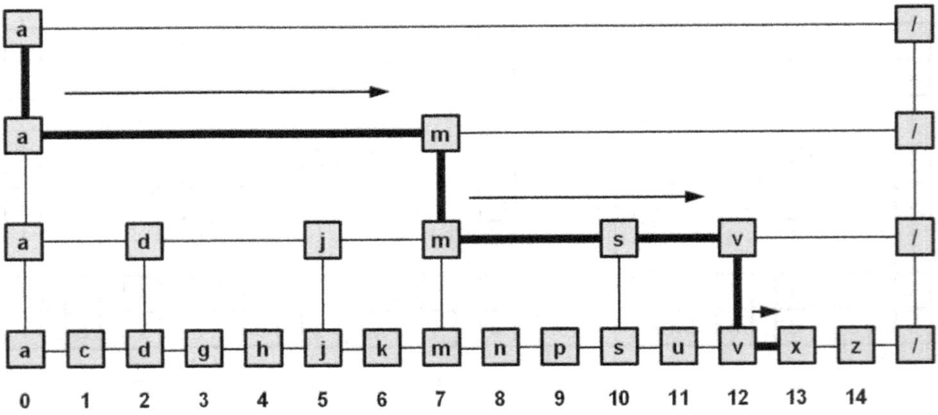

Figure 3.8: A basic level linked B+-tree that supports an efficient ordered set or dictionary. The internal nodes of the tree store keys of elements only. The path formed by thick links illustrates the top-down search for the node at the deepest level that contains element x.

The search for a rank and search for a key are very similar top-down algorithms (see Figure 3.3 and Figure 3.8). For the best performance, they find the shortest path from the root of a tree. The difference is that the search for a key involves comparisons only, while the search operations on counts use the addition and comparison with an accumulated value. In this respect, the search for a key is simpler than the search for a rank. Both searches guarantee the same logarithmic running time.

The combination of two datasets in one data structure offers the functionality not achievable with separate basic data structures. The first advantage is the extension of the variety of fast primary algorithms. The augmented level linked B+-tree for ordered sequences (see Figure 3.7) supports fast operations on both ranks and keys. The second advantage is that an algorithm can provide more information in response to client needs. The advanced algorithms can be implemented so that one search algorithm computes its matching search parameter. For example, the search for an element associated with a given key returns not only the element but also its rank. This extended variant is useful in range queries, since reporting the number of elements between two positions found takes constant time only. In basic linked data structures, the running time is linear in the distance between the positions.

The generality of the method of augmenting enable us to improve performance of various types of basic data structures. The diagrams shown in this section are similar to diagrams of augmented red-black and binary search trees. In all of these trees, a node stores the size of a sub-tree. Although the result is the same, the purpose of augmenting a data structure can be interpreted differently. Here, we modify a B+-tree, which supports an efficient sequence, in order to add fast search for a key. We prefer this approach, since our interest is in summation algorithms, which are defined for sequences regardless of whether they are ordered or not. For classical search trees, which support sets and dictionaries, the efficient rank algorithm is introduced as an additional feature for the purpose of improving performance of order statistics. The aspect of applying this method to obtain unordered sequences is not normally discussed.

Quite obviously, there is no fundamental restriction that would disallow using these augmented trees for the representation of unordered sequences. The augmented red-black trees are particularly attractive alternative to arrays in applications, which require a wide range of efficient insertion, deletion and search operations. Given an implementation of a red-black tree that supports an ordered sequence, it is not too challenging to develop a variant for an unordered sequence. The fast rank algorithm plus the inorder traversal algorithm provide adequate facilities for both types of fast sequences. The requirements for ordered sequences are stricter, because insertions must keep such a sequence sorted. Unordered sequences do not place this restriction. Many new operations can be obtained from matching operations for ordered sequences. Although this might be a bit challenging for a novice, experienced programmers usually write variants of augmented red-black trees, which support both ordered and unordered sequences.

For the fast sequential summation algorithms discussed in the next chapter, the order of elements is not important unless numerical errors cause accuracy issues. To simplify explanation and diagrams, we avoid using ordered sequences later in this book.

	Linked List	Array	Red-Black Tree	Augmented B+-Tree
Search	$O(N)$	$O(\log N)$	$O(\log N)$	$O(\log N)$
Insertion	$O(1)$	$O(N)$	$O(\log N)$	$O(\log N)$
Deletion	$O(1)$	$O(N)$	$O(\log N)$	$O(\log N)$
Range Query	$O(K)$	$O(1)$	$O(K)$	$O(1)$
Rank	$O(R)$	$O(1)$	$O(R)$	$O(\log N)$

Table 3.2: The computational complexities of primary operations of ordered sequences and sets based on basic data structures and an augmented B+-tree. Linked list uses sequential search, ordered array uses binary search. Range query operation - count the number of elements. N is the number of elements in a given dataset. K is the number of elements in a range. Rank - retrieve an element at a given rank R.

3.12 ALTERNATIVES TO BASIC DATA STRUCTURES

In this section, we concentrate on the typical performance issues of basic data structures used for the representation of a mathematical sequence and benefits offered by advanced data structures. Although these issues are discussed in the context of requirements for processing large datasets, they are not unusual in smaller scale applications.

The essential aspect of these performance issues is that they are closely related to the generality of a sequence representation. Since there is a tradeoff between the cost of development and the benefit of a result, there are many ways of using advanced data structures in practical applications. The simple programming solutions directly use primary algorithms of data structures. This is acceptable for small size projects and programming solutions. The well-known drawback of this approach is the complexity of a user algorithm associated with the implementation details of specific data structures. As the size of a project increases, it is more practical to choose a higher level of abstraction of a programming solution. For advanced data structures, this is important not only to address the issue of the complexity of the code but also to achieve the optimal performance. These benefits are much more significant than for basic data structures.

For the analysis, the number of primary operations and the number of data structures have been reduced to smallest possible. We omit efficient operations on ends of linear structures, which are useful in practice, but do not support general purpose solutions. Our interest is in the worst case performance. The operations listed in Table 3.1 and Table 3.2 have been selected in the context of our minimal requirement for processing large datasets. Despite small size, this set of operations is sufficient to illustrate the frequent performance problems that arise in practical applications.

The demo variants of the problems discussed here and in textbooks have simple formulations. Dealing with these problems in practice can be much more complicated task, since there are significant challenges in complex software products. The first one is finding the code and methods that cause a performance issue. And this can take more time than implementing a solution. For a novice, the cause of such problems often comes as a big surprise.

The interesting reason why these performance issues arise is the success of a software product. There is no need to worry about bad products, they simply disappear. Instead, our attention should be focused on successful products, because they evolve in response to customer's requests. The standard situation is that the first successful version of a product is small and simple. The subsequent improvements make it large and complex. This product evolution has unavoidable effect on the overall performance.

At the level of algorithms, the most typical enhancement requests are: increase the size of a user dataset or add a new operation on the data. The structural complexity of a user input can also change dramatically over time. Each of these requests involves the risk of performance degradation. The usual and significant complication is that at the time of the development programmers do not know what changes to a product are to come. The new specific operations and their frequencies are unknown parameters of a model. This is the practical reason why we need the worst case analysis of algorithms. As the size of a problem and its internal complexity increase, fine tuning implementation becomes more challenging and time consuming.

These performance issues are serious enough to write chapters in books and to consider developing advanced data structures that address these issues. They are often responsible for the cost of development, which is unaffordable in the competitive software market. Because of high complexity of specific applications, dealing with these issues is much more challenging than solving textbook exercises. When programmers fail, it requires expert involvement to re-design a business model and/or a mathematical solution. The delay of a product release may lead to undesirable and serious consequences.

It is well known that primary algorithms of basic data structure have different performance characteristics (see Table 2.2). This dissimilarity complicates the development of algorithms for complex applications. The most reasonable approach to address this issue is to design and implement unified interfaces, which are supported by underlying data structures. The goal is to make these data structures interchangeable. This approach enables a user algorithm to easily address a performance issue by switching from one representation to another. This is cost effective, since the improvements are achieved without rewriting complex user algorithms. For this reason, the high quality libraries offer wide choices of data structures. The documentation provides explanations of how to choose the best data structure for a specific application. The recommendations are based on the frequency of operations required in a user algorithm. For example, use an array for efficient data processing or use a linked list to insert or delete a large number of elements in the middle of a sequence. It is important to note that these recommendations are based on the best case performance of operations. In other words, these recommendations use optimistic estimates.

The approach of interchangeable data structures is quite effective in relatively simple applications that use a small number of primary operations, since the variety of library data structures is wide enough to implement an efficient solution. However, real-life problems are rarely simple. As the number of operations required in a user algorithm increases, the choice of suitable data structures narrows.

As an illustration of the fundamental weakness of classical data structures, consider an algorithm of incremental construction of an ordered sequence, which uses two primary operations: search and insert. Note that the search operation involves moving to the position of inserting a new element. Given a random input, the performance of such a construction is quadratic regardless of whether we choose an array or a linked list. An array provides fast random access, but slow insertion, whereas a linked list provides fast insertion, but slow random access. Both classical data structures cause performance degradation of this user algorithm. This fact implies that the method of swapping representations does not work in this relatively simple but very important practical application, since user datasets grow and shrink. And this is an interesting problem, because the performance characteristics of arrays and linked lists complement each other (see Table 3.1). In theory, if there was a working combination, it would provide the most efficient representation of a sequence.

This performance problem of the classical data structures is solved with an augmented level linked B+-tree, which supports both efficient search and efficient insertion (see Table 3.1). The tree reduces the running time of the incremental construction from quadratic to linearithmic ($N \log N$). This simple example demonstrates the significant potential of advanced data structures for performance improvements in practical applications.

Unlike sequences, it is much easier to achieve high efficiency of a programming solution for a set-based mathematical model, because balanced search trees have logarithmic running time of both search and insert operations. In particular, there is no need to use advanced data structures in the incremental construction of an ordered set. A balanced search tree provides acceptable performance, whereas an array-based ordered set is not suitable due to linear performance of insert operation. Unfortunately, these basic trees become too slow when a user algorithm needs additional sequence facilities. Not only random access is inefficient, but also simple operation of determining the number of elements in a range takes linear time. An augmented level linked B+-tree offers the best variety of efficient operations (see Table 3.2) for applications that requires both set and sequence facilities.

The performance problems caused by arrays deserve a bit more detailed discussion, since in modern computer systems they are superior to linked data structures in algorithms for small problems. Because of this superiority, arrays are very popular choice for the development of prototypes. This particular use of arrays in industrial projects is not always safe and may become a burden due to strict delivery deadlines. A prototype, which becomes the first commercial release of a product, is one of the biggest traps in the future. As the size of a problem increases, the array operations with linear running time dramatically slow down a user algorithm. Not surprisingly, this simple property of arrays is the most frequent reason for performance issues in many modern programming solutions. For the same reason, the analysis of complex algorithms should start with the code that uses the slow array operations. Profilers and debuggers help us find the most significant contributions to the total running time, which should be fixed first. However, the software development tools do not provide insight into the design of complex algorithms. Solving these performance problems requires significant effort of reverse engineering, which is challenging even for well documented code.

Although basic data structures can support a wide range of operations of a unified interface, in terms of performance, they remain specialized. The generality and efficiency is not achievable with basic data structures only, because one inefficient operation in a complex user algorithm leads to serious performance degradation. The blind search for a suitable data structure can be a waste of time. As we have seen before, there is no good choice even for relatively simple practical applications. But the advantage of unified interfaces is that they significantly reduce the time needed to come to this conclusion and start looking for an alternative solution.

The number of methods to deal with the performance issues caused by basic data structures is actually not so big. If a library provides interchangeable data structures with unified interfaces, it is designed with the potential to cover new applications areas. In this case, it makes sense to consider at first the library extension based on advanced data structures, such as augmented trees. The ideal general purpose data structure does not have inefficient operations at all. In reality, it is sufficient to add to the library only data structures with efficient operations required in user algorithms. Provided that the new data structures support specified interfaces, they can easily replace inefficient basic data structures in existing programming solutions.

Without the general purpose advanced data structures, the only remaining method is the development of specific solutions, which is impossible without professional knowledge of a business area and high skills of programmers. With this method, the complexity of a problem is reflected in the complexity of the solutions and the size of the implementation code. Non-reusable bulky algorithms come with the spiraling cost of development and maintenance. For large projects, the benefits of advanced data structures become quite substantial to be ignored. Even home-grown variants would be quite useful. The cost of development of such data structures will be more than compensated by the ease of addressing performance issues.

Which advanced data structures to choose for a general purpose library is not a trivial design decision, because the class of advanced data structures is considerably wider than the class of basic data structures. The high quality library achieves a tradeoff between the size of facilities and the size of implementation code. Here, we briefly consider the following two design aspects, which are important for each library: the performance and the generality as the ability to support high level abstractions and modelling. In both of these aspects, a library can have significant benefits from using advanced data structures.

In the context of performance, there is no need in maintaining many data structures that offer duplicate facilities with close performance. It is more important to consider data structures that provide operations more efficient than arrays, because they are frequently used in many types of applications and may lead to performance issues that are difficult to address.

In terms of generality, the design of a library aims at a high level of abstraction. This goal is achieved with abstract data types that define unified interfaces and hide complex representation details from user algorithms. A top level abstract data type represents a mathematical concept or an abstract data structure. Each library offers a broad spectrum of abstract data types. In addition to sequences and sets, which are in the main focus of this chapter, a library provides other important abstract data types, such as stack, queue and priority queue.

The augmented B+-trees have the attractive property for the implementation of the general purpose libraries. They provide more efficient primary operations than any basic data structure. This implies that such a B+-tree can support several interfaces, which usually require a number of different basic data structures. The wider variety of efficient primary operations offered by an advanced data structure, the smaller total number of data structures is needed to support all of the library interfaces.

The wide set of efficient operations supported by one data structure is the key to achieving performance, high level of generality and keeping the size of a library optimal. While basic data structures offer fixed facilities, advanced data structures have the flexibility in adding new efficient operations by applying the method of augmenting.

3.13 ARRAY-BASED B+-TREES

In this chapter, we used for the explanation of key ideas level linked B+-trees. The main reason for this choice is that the diagrams of linked data structures are quite effective in the analysis and design of algorithms. The array-based representations of the same trees are less suitable for this purpose because they are implicit and do not show clearly basic components of a structure and their relationships. At the same time, the array-based B+-trees, including their level linked and augmented variants, offer important practical advantages. They are more space efficient than link-based variants of the same trees, since arrays are superior to linked lists in terms of access operations and do not need to store links to previous and next nodes. As a result, they offer much better performance that comes from fast pointer arithmetic and improved locality of reference. A client can gain the benefit of fast access and array specific algorithms instead of sequential search and algorithms on chains of linked nodes.

One of the options to develop an array-based B+-tree is to borrow an external search tree and replace its data scheme with a new one appropriate for a user application. The other option that saves development time is to start with an available implementation of a level linked B+-tree. In this case, an equivalent array-based variant can be obtained using the simple conversion method. Each linked list of one group of siblings is replaced by a dynamic array with a fixed capacity. Because of high efficiency of operations on small size arrays, it is often sufficient to apply this conversion method to the deepest level only. In this variant of a B+-tree, the deepest level represents a linked list of dynamic arrays (see Figure 3.9).

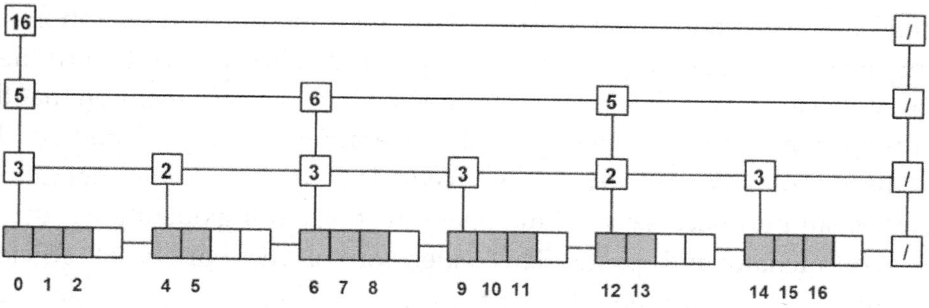

Figure 3.9: Illustration of storage facilities of an array-based B+-tree with the structure equivalent to that in Figure 3.5. The deepest level of the tree can be viewed as a partition of an array (a given sequence of 17 elements) into a list of 6 subarrays. The internal nodes store counts of sequence elements.

The substantial difference in the efficiency of operations on arrays and chains of linked nodes is a potential complication for achieving the optimal performance of such a hybrid data structure. In order to overcome this problem, this variant of a B+-tree introduces a branching factor for siblings stored in arrays of the deepest levels. The value of this parameter can be one to two orders of magnitude greater than that for internal levels. The increase in the size of one group of siblings proportionally reduces the number of internal (dynamically allocated) nodes and, thus, the height of a tree. These structural changes improve performance of sequential processing and search operations but adversely affect the running time of insertions and deletions. The general purpose variants of these trees are fine-tuned in terms of overall performance.

The classical example of an unordered and non-numeric sequence is a string of characters. Figure 3.10 shows an example of a string using the array-based B+-tree discussed above. This representation is optimized for editing large texts. It can deliver significant performance improvements by replacing an array-based string, which is the first choice for this type of applications. Because of the partition into subarrays, the new representation provides a bit slower sequential and random access than an array that stores characters in memory contiguously. The key strength of the new representation of a string is the high performance of modifying operations. The list of these operations includes insertions and deletions of single characters and, what is particularly relevant, efficient operations on large texts and substrings: split and join. The detailed description of these operations is beyond the scope of this book. Here, we only mention that the running time of these two primary operations is logarithmic in the maximum of sizes of strings involved. The split and join operations provide support necessary to implement the text editing operations such as cut, concatenate and paste. This extension of the variety of efficient operations is a substantial boost to the performance in large scale applications.

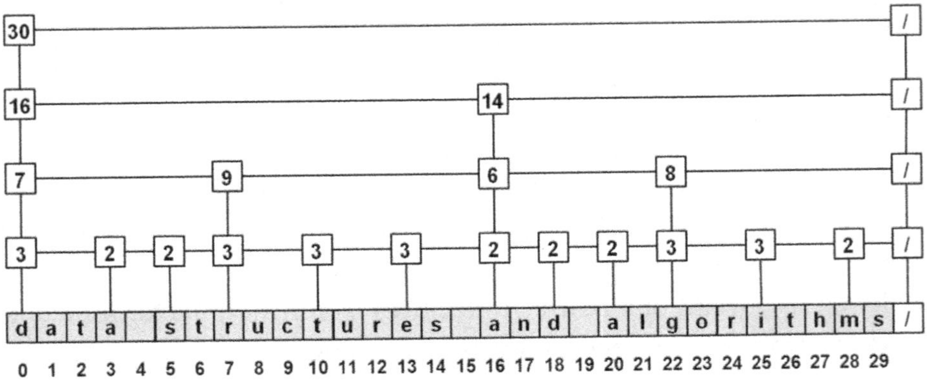

Figure 3.10: A string using an array-based variant of a B+-tree shown in Figure 3.9. The diagram removed empty cells from subarrays of the deepest level.

The well-known data structure that offers practically the same efficient facilities for text editing applications is called a rope. This fact may be surprising, but it can be understood if we notice that a rope has data organization similar to our array-based B+-tree (Figure 3.9 and Figure 3.10). The external nodes store arrays of characters, and internal nodes store counts of characters in sub-trees. The main difference is that a rope uses for efficient navigation a basic (not level linked) binary tree, which has the fixed small branching factor. Because of this feature, a rope does not have the same flexibility as a B+-tree for optimizing the performance of primary operations.

3.14 SUMMARY

In this chapter, we have described the representation of a mathematical sequence based on augmented level linked B+-trees, which outperform basic data structures in complex user algorithms. The representation offers sequential and random access with the efficiency close to that in arrays but significantly faster insert and delete operations. For this reason, it provides a valuable alternative to an array or a linked list in many practical applications.

The high performance of this variant of B+-trees is achieved using the combination of a level linked B-tree and a linked list that provides the best performance characteristics of each constituent data structure. From the practical perspective, it is important that the two-dimensional structure of linear chains of level linked B+-trees enables simple implementations of primary algorithms for search, insertion and deletion. The tree can store not only data elements provided by a user but also various representation specific data associated with structural invariants and the user dataset. Storing the additional data is highly space efficient, since they are added only to internal nodes of such a B+-tree. These storage facilities are optimal for the method of augmenting that allows us to design new efficient algorithms by inserting new types of data into internal nodes of the level linked B+-trees.

One of the key differences between an array and a sequence based on an augmented level linked B+-tree can be summarized as follows. An array is equipped with the subscript operator, which is directly supported by a programming language. An augmented level linked tree has a special sub-structure of counts with the fast search and counting methods to access an element specified by its rank.

Here, we discussed only several primary algorithms on augmented level linked B+-trees. In a broader context of processing large datasets, linked data structures have the following important advantage over arrays. They offer efficient split, cut and join (concatenate) operations. The high efficiency of these operations is achieved by changing connectivity between a small number of nodes of data structures involved. The implementations of these operations on linked lists are particularly simple and guarantee constant running time. A balanced tree provides logarithmic performance. The running time of these operations on the augmented level linked B+-trees described in this book is logarithmic too. The array implementations of these operations are inefficient because of copying elements from one array into another.

The main focus of this chapter is on the performance. The solutions to complex problems significantly benefit from data structures with wide variety of algorithms that support high levels of abstraction and generality. Unlike basic data structures, such as arrays and lists, the advanced data structures offer the flexibility in adding new efficient operations by applying the method of augmenting. They can represent not only sequences but also other mathematical concepts and abstract data types.

The development of an advanced data structure is not a trivial task. The order of the description of algorithms in this chapter is close to that we use in practice. We start with the simplest construction algorithm either incremental or from a given dataset. Since most data structures provide symmetrical facilities, we add the inverse operation of emptying the whole data structure or deleting a single element. When the acceptable quality is achieved and the operations maintain specified invariants, we can add various types of searches for an element associated with a given rank or key. The next stage is the implementation of more complex efficient algorithms.

The complexity and potentially large size of implementation code imply that a programming language should provide adequate facilities for the development of the data structures described in this chapter. In terms of the cost of development and maintenance, the minimal requirement is the support for object-oriented programming technique. The first implementations of these data structures are written for concrete types. The subsequent versions benefit from using parameterized types offered by the generic programming technique. Switching from concrete to parameterized types is more beneficial at earlier rather than later stages of the development.

Chapter 4: Summation

In everyday work, we do not notice the fundamental importance of summation algorithms. We just use them as simple and reliable tools to solve problems and answer queries. These algorithms are vital to a wide range of applications from scientific to commercial. They pass through every level of practical use of computers in data processing and analysis. The computation of the main statistical characteristics of datasets, such as the mean and the standard deviation, is only one important application of summation algorithms.

Many types of applications deal with constantly growing volumes of data and, thus, require the increasing computational power of systems. The linear running time of the standard sequential summation on basic data structures is acceptable for processing of small datasets, but it becomes performance bottleneck for large and huge datasets. Any improvement in the running time of summation algorithms is very beneficial for such applications. The need for such improvements is a compelling reason to look for alternative algorithms and approaches.

The issue of linear running time can be easily addressed in simple applications. The method is based on an auxiliary array, which stores pre-computed partial sums for a given sequence. With such a special array, the sum of consecutive elements in the range $[m, n)$ is computed in constant time as the difference between the sum of the first n elements and the sum of the first m elements. The disadvantage of this method is that it is not efficient in the general case. In particular, a user can modify the value of an element in the given sequence. This is a constant time operation on a basic data structure that represents the sequence. However, this simple operation makes invalid the array of pre-computed sums and updating this array takes linear time. The solution comes at the price of another problem: Having two data structures with different types of inefficient operations in a user algorithm involves the risk of degradation in the overall performance.

In this chapter, we extend the requirements for efficient processing of large datasets by including new operations. The main focus is on the sequential summation algorithms that provide logarithmic performance. It is important that, in contrast to parallel algorithms, these sequential algorithms guarantee both logarithmic running time and logarithmic total number of operations. In terms of equivalent hardware upgrade, this is a huge improvement over algorithms on basic data structures and parallel algorithms.

The fast sequential summation algorithms are not only important for practical applications. They are also interesting from the design perspective. This chapter illustrates the power of the method of augmenting in the development of new efficient algorithms. Unlike well-known comparison-based algorithms on balanced search trees, the new algorithms operate on accumulated values. We apply this method to the data structure that already supports a mathematical sequence described in Chapter 3. This is why, the new algorithms are introduced without loss of efficiency of other primary operations, such as search, insertion and deletion.

One of the interesting questions that arises in the design of algorithms is why some obvious ideas work on arrays and do not work on linked data structures? This chapter aims to help better understand the important differences between linked and array representations of data structures. Although the discussion concentrates on linked data structures, the knowledge is useful even if the reader is planning to write algorithms based on arrays only.

4.1 PARTIAL SUM

By definition, *N*th partial sum is the sum of the first *N* values in a given sequence. The straightforward computation of this sum takes linear time and represents one of the simplest summation algorithms. Most programming implementations of these algorithms use zero-based indexing. In this case, the definition of a partial sum

$$S_n = \sum_{i=0}^{n-1} a_i$$

is usually expressed as a variant of the following algorithm

```
int sum = 0;
for (int k=0; k<N; ++k)
    sum = sum + a[k];
```

One-based indexing is another indexing frequently used in programming solutions. The corresponding definition of a partial sum

$$S_n = \sum_{i=1}^{n} a_i$$

has a typical implementation, such as shown below

```
int sum = 0;
for (int k=1; k<=N; ++k)
    sum = sum + a[k];
```

We start with the design of the data structure that supports much more efficient computation of the sum of the first consecutive values in a sequence. One of the reasons for this choice is that this is probably the simplest fast summation algorithm. Another reason is that this algorithm in some aspects is similar to the fast top-down rank algorithm described in Chapter 3. We can borrow useful ideas to develop the new summation algorithm.

To highlight the ideas that help us design the required data structure and efficient algorithm, let us consider the specific example: the summation of six values of a sequence. For comparison, we show the computation of the rank of the last element, which represents the trivial sum of six values equal to one.

rank: 1 + 1 + 1 + 1 + 1 + 1;

sum: A1 +A2 +A3 +A4 +A5 +A6;

The similarity between these two algorithms is quite evident. Both algorithms apply the same operation of the addition. The difference is in specific values the algorithms operate on. The summation algorithm supersedes the rank algorithm, since the former can be applied to arbitrary values, whereas the latter only to the values equal to one. Because of its algebraic generality, the summation algorithm normally makes unnecessary the simple arithmetic rank algorithm.

However, for our task of developing a fast summation algorithm both algorithms and their similarity are important. Figure 4.1 shows a data structure that provides the fast top-down rank algorithm. It based on efficient counting that breaks the barrier of linear performance, which is the same as that of the sequential summation on basic data structures.

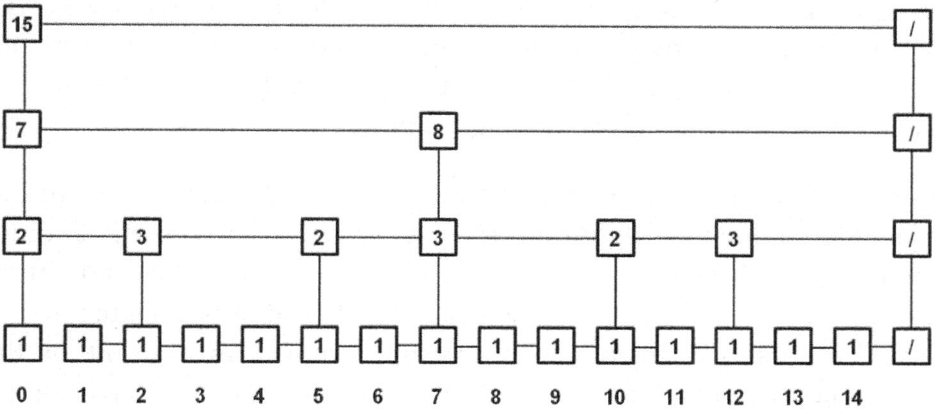

Figure 4.1: A level linked B+-tree that stores in internal nodes counts of sequence elements and supports the fast top-down rank algorithm.

The idea is simple: to use the fast rank algorithm as a prototype for the development of the fast general purpose summation algorithm. If this idea is correct, we expect that such an algorithm will have logarithmic performance. At this stage, it seems that the easiest way to achieve this goal is to remove the restriction on the operand value and to allow the addition to operate on arbitrary values. Let us now consider this idea in detail.

The fast top-down rank algorithm finds an element specified by a given rank. It implements not only efficient search but also efficient summation of counts of elements in a sequence. The main attractive feature of this algorithm is that it significantly reduces the number of addition operations required to compute the rank value. If we apply the same method to the summation problem, we should obtain the fast summation algorithm. The only remaining issue is that the rank algorithm does not support the general purpose summation, since it places the restriction that each value be equal to one.

How significant is this restriction?

In the context of the development of efficient computer algorithms, the main restriction is imposed not by the value of an operand, but by the computational cost of a single operation of the addition of two values. Any computer type meets the requirements for the fast summation algorithms discussed in this chapter provided that the addition of two values is a constant time operation. Modern computer systems and programming languages provide many suitable built-in types and facilities to add user defined types for solving a wide range of practical problems.

Thus, we may obtain the advanced data structure that supports an efficient sequential summation algorithm, if we choose a type with the addition operation, which takes constant time. And use values of this type in the data structure, which supports the fast rank algorithm (see Figure 4.1), to replace counts of elements with matching sums. As a result of this extension of the data structure for the fast rank algorithm, we arrive at the data structure shown in Figure 4.2.

Each internal node of this data structure stores the sum of values of its child nodes, which is equal to the sum of all of the values of the elements in a sub-tree rooted at this internal node. Since the values of sums replaced the values of counts of elements, the new data structure of sums represents a more general variant of the data structure of counts of elements, but not counts of children.

The similarity with the data structure of counts of elements implies that many algorithms discussed before can be easily adapted to the new data structure. In particular, such a data structure can be efficiently built using the bottom-up construction algorithm from a given dataset or the incremental construction operations of insertions.

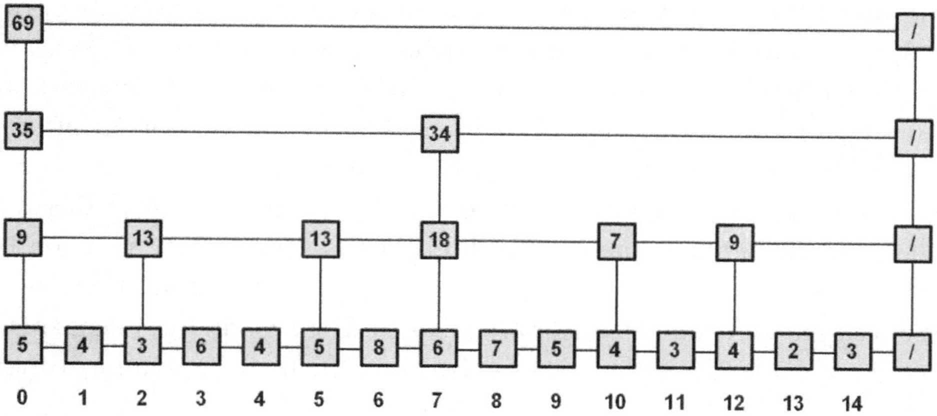

Figure 4.2: A level linked B+-tree that stores a given sequence in nodes of the deepest level and sums of consecutive values in internal nodes. It has the same structure as the tree in Figure 4.1 and can be viewed as an extension, which is obtained by removing the restriction that each value is equal to one.

The new data structure of sums has the capacity to support fast summation, because it can avoid unnecessary re-computations by using values of sums of large numbers of values saved in internal nodes. To complete the design of a fast summation algorithm, we need to take advantage of these data.

The mathematical rules of summation are formulated for sequences. The limits of summation are specified through the ranks of consecutive elements to be processed. The partial sum algorithm is particularly simple, since it needs to know only the upper limit of summation, which is equal to the number of the first elements in a given sequence.

However, the data structure of sums (see Figure 4.2) does not store counts of sequence elements. Finding the upper limit of summation and/or the last element to be processed takes linear time, because an algorithm must count all of the elements it processes. Without the dataset that supports the efficient rank method, a summation algorithm cannot efficiently identify the elements to be processed. The data structure of sums offers sequence facilities equivalent to those of a basic data structure, such as a linked list.

The straightforward implementation of the idea of the extension of the fast rank algorithm by removing the restriction of a fixed value of 1 does not work, because the new data structure of sums does not support fast counting of processed elements and thus cannot represent an efficient general purpose sequence. The required facilities have been lost as a result of the generalization applied to the original data structure. And this is an interesting issue of a sequence, which is often unexpected for a novice. For comparison, there is no such performance issue in applications using balanced search trees for sets or dictionaries. The first and last elements of a range of consecutive elements can be found by their keys in logarithmic time.

At the same time, efficient random access to elements by itself does not guarantee the high performance of summation algorithms. Without proper facilities, neither an array nor a balanced tree augmented with counts of elements can deliver performance of summation better than linear.

This means that the data structure of sums (see Figure 4.2) and the data structure of counts, which supports an efficient general purpose sequence (see Figure 4.1), do not provide adequate facilities separately. In order to develop the fast sequential summation algorithm, we need a data structure, which is more complex than each of these data structures.

The solution to the problem caused by inefficiencies of different operations and facilities is to store two datasets for different purposes in one data structure. In this particular case, this is possible, since both datasets are associated with the same structure of linked nodes. Such a new complex data structure (see Figure 4.3) represents a combination of the data structures of counts and sums shown in Figure 4.1 and Figure 4.2. It has the ability to efficiently support the summation operations and the rank algorithm, because internal nodes of this data structure store both sums of consecutive values in a sequence and counts of these values. One of the ways to view the effect of this combination is that adding counts of values to the data structure of sums transforms this data structure into an efficient sequence.

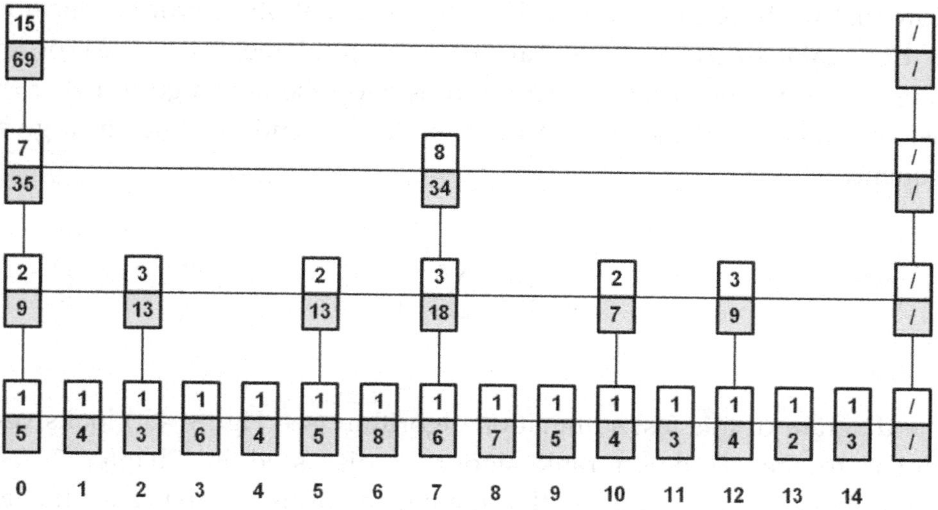

Figure 4.3: A level linked B+-tree that provides efficient facilities for a general purpose sequence and fast summation algorithms. The tree is a combination of the trees shown in Figure 4.1 and Figure 4.2. Its internal nodes store both counts and sums of consecutive values.

In theory, the sub-structure of sums supersedes the sub-structure of counts. When each value of a given sequence is equal to one, these two datasets associated with internal nodes become identical. Despite this fact, the sub-structure of sums is not designed to replace the sub-structure of counts. These sub-structures complement each other in the fast summation algorithms. They store two different datasets that support different efficient primary operations of complex algorithms. This approach optimizes the performance by allowing a user algorithm to choose the most efficient specific operations. A fast sequential summation algorithm involves the facilities of both sub-structures.

The sub-structure of counts of elements stores only non-negative integers. It supports the fast top-down rank algorithm, which is critical to the efficient representation of a mathematical sequence. This sub-structure offers efficient navigation facilities for finding elements to be processed by a summation algorithm. The sub-structure of sums can store elements of any type that support the constant time addition operation, for example, complex numbers.

Now that we have the complex data structure that offers efficient facilities of two data structures, we can properly implement the idea of the extension of the fast rank algorithm to develop the new algorithm for the fast computation of the sum of the first *N* consecutive values in a given sequence

$$S_n = \sum_{i=0}^{n-1} a_i$$

The diagram of this fast summation algorithm (see Figure 4.4) looks very similar to the top-down rank algorithm discussed in Chapter 3. The similarity comes from the fact that the new algorithm searches for the last sequence element to be processed. The upper limit of summation provides the rank of the last element. The algorithm starts at the first node at the top level and moves to the node at the deepest level that stores the last

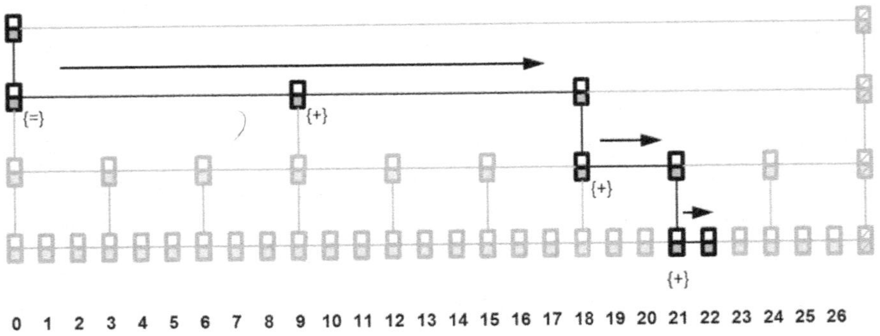

Figure 4.4: Illustration of the fast partial sum algorithm using a shortest path detected by the top-down search for a node at the deepest level with a given rank. A pre-computed sum or a value is associated with a horizontal link. The first operation is the initialization by the assignment operator. The algorithm performs 4 operations to compute the sum of the first 21 values.

element. The extension feature of this summation algorithm is the new variable, which represents the total sum of values of processed sequence elements. The total sum is updated simultaneously with the total count of processed elements, when the search moves forward by traversing a horizontal link to a next node. Thus, the summation algorithm performs two types of the addition of counts and sums of values stored in visited nodes.

The shortest path of the top-down rank algorithm guarantees the optimal performance of this summation algorithm. It is logarithmic if the addition is a constant time operation. In the most general description, this fast summation algorithm represents a shortest path algorithm that accumulates values of sums in visited nodes.

The algorithm for the fast computation of a partial sum could be illustrated using the extended code for the efficient top-down rank algorithm (see Chapter 3). However, since an augmented B+-tree that supports efficient summation stores an additional type of accumulated data, saving space becomes more important for practical applications. Thus, we will consider a more realistic variant of the algorithm, which uses two types of nodes.

Given an internal node that stores connectivity and accumulated data

```
struct NodeInternal
{
    // pointer to next node
    NodeInternalPointer next;
    // pointer to node one level down
    NodeInternalPointer down;
    // size of sub-tree
    int count;
    // sum of all values in sub-tree
    int sum;
    ...
};
```

and a node for the list of the deepest level

```
struct NodeDeep
{
    // pointer to next node
    NodeDeepPointer next;
    // sequence value
    int value;
    ...
};
```

the following pseudo-code illustrates the algorithm for the fast computation of a partial sum specified by the rank of the last value:

```
// partial sum to be computed
int sum = 0;
// count of processed values
int count = 0;
// start processing at
// first node of top level
NodeInternalPointer p_node = p_top_start;

// process internal nodes
while ( p_node->down!=0 )
{
    // compute sum at one internal level
    while ( (count+p_node->count)<=rank )
    {
        // add count
        count = count + p_node->count;
        // add accumulated value
        sum = sum + p_node->sum;
        // move forward
        p_node = p_node->next;
    }

    // move down one level
    p_node = p_node->down;
}

// pointer to node of the deepest level
NodeDeepPointer p_deep(p_node);

// process the deepest level
while ( count<rank )
{
    // add current value
    sum = sum + p_deep->value;
    // increment count
    ++count;
    // move forward
    p_deep = p_deep->next;
}

return sum;
```

This algorithm has quite simple structure and interpretation if we replace summation at each level by one resulting value

```
sum_partial = sum_level_1+sum_level_2+...+sum_level_H;
```

A sum at each level is the sum of the values in a large range of a given sequence. The number of levels and, thus, sums are logarithmic in the size of a sequence.

It is also important to emphasize that summation in this algorithm parallels counting processed elements:

```
while ( (count+p_node->count)<rank )
{
    // add count
    count = count + p_node->count;
    // add accumulated value
    sum = sum + p_node->sum;
    // move forward
    p_node = p_node->next;
}
```

In this section, we developed the fast partial sum algorithm by extending the top-down rank algorithm and combining two datasets in one data structure. Alternatively, we could introduce such an algorithm by augmenting the general representation of a sequence described in Chapter 3. When we start with an unordered sequence, we add to each internal node the sum of all of the values of elements in the sub-tree rooted at the node and arrive at the same data structure as shown in Figure 4.3. We have used this approach of adding new implementation specific data to internal nodes in Chapter 3 to design the level linked B+-tree, which represents an ordered sequence.

However, since the combined data structure looks a bit complex, the natural question arises whether it can be simplified. Why do we need the sub-structure of counts of elements, when we already have the more general sub-structure of sums? Why not to reduce the complexity of this data structure by removing the "redundant" sub-structure of counts?

These questions help clarify the important difference between representations using a linked data structure and an array. The sub-structure of counts of elements is unnecessary for array-based representations that offer fast random access to any element. For a linked data structure, it is essential to maintain the sub-structure of counts of sequence elements. Without such a sub-structure the representation loses the high efficiency of sequence facilities.

4.2 SUM OF CONSECUTIVE VALUES

In many applications, it is necessary to compute the sum of values in any given range of consecutive elements of a sequence, not just first ones.

$$S_{[m,n)} = \sum_{i=m}^{n-1} a_i$$

Theoretically, the fast partial sum algorithm is sufficient to compute such a sum. For a given range [***m***, ***n***), the result is obtained by subtracting the sum of the first ***m*** values from the sum of the first ***n*** values.

$$S_{[m,n)} = S_n - S_m$$

This method looks attractive, since it is simple and enables us to obtain the result in time logarithmic in the number of elements in a sequence. Moreover, an augmented B+-tree addresses the performance issues of an array of pre-computed partial sums by providing efficient operations that insert, delete and update values in a sequence. One augmented tree has the ability to replace several supporting basic data structures in a complex algorithm. It helps us to avoid complications associated with different performance of operations on the supporting data structures. Nevertheless, in applications processing large datasets, this simple method should be used with care to avoid potential problems associated with inaccuracy of numerical computations.

The mathematical method assumes that a numeric type supports exact arithmetic. This is not achievable with floating point numbers, which provide approximate representation of real numbers. The loss of precision occurs when the sum of values before a given range is significantly larger than the sum of values in the range. The choice of an integer type avoids rounding errors and guarantees exact arithmetic operations of addition and subtraction. However, this safety comes at the expense of dealing with the problems of overflow and space loss associated with the increase in the size of the integer type to improve precision.

Another drawback of this method of computing the sum of consecutive values follows from the facts that the sum of the values before a given range is computed twice and these computations are useless, since the sum makes no contribution to the result. For a small range, this method is less effective than the straightforward sequential summation.

These issues of the fast partial sum algorithm demonstrate the need in an alternative efficient algorithm more suitable for practical applications. As discussed in Chapter 3, the level linked B+-trees support two efficient search algorithms for sequence elements specified by ranks: top-down search and finger search. The second algorithm has the property, which is instrumental for the development of the required fast summation algorithm. It implements the highly efficient local search that passes through the internal nodes optimally connected to the nodes of deepest level with the sequence elements.

At this stage, it is not too challenging to devise the new fast summation algorithm, because now we have the data structure that supports one fast summation algorithm. In order to obtain the required summation algorithm, we apply to this data structure the same method that helped us develop the fast partial sum algorithm. As a result, the new algorithm for fast summation of consecutive values represents the extension of the finger search algorithm (see Figure 4.5). This summation algorithm uses the path detected by finger search to sum up values of elements in visited nodes at the deepest level and sums in internal nodes.

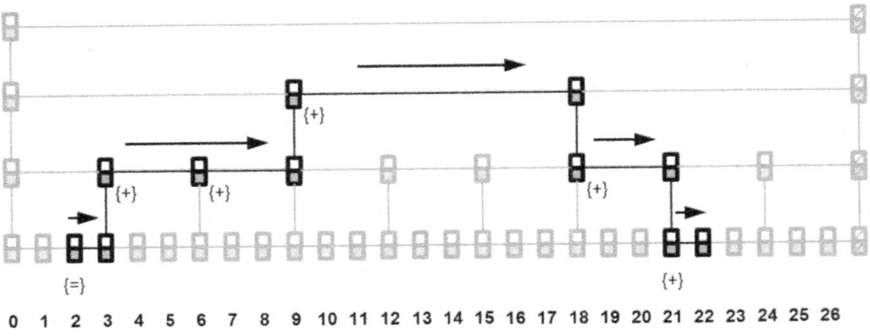

Figure 4.5: Illustration of the fast summation algorithm using a shortest path between two nodes of the deepest level detected by finger search. A pre-computed sum or a value is associated with a horizontal link. The first operation is the initialization by the assignment operator. The algorithm performs 6 operations to compute the sum of 20 values in the range [2, 22).

The lower and upper summation limits provide the ranks of the first and last elements to be processed and, thus, the start and end nodes of the deepest level. Moving from the first to the last element through the deepest level, which stores all of the elements of a given sequence, is not efficient. This method provides the path of the standard sequential summation on a linked list. The length of this path is linear in the number of consecutive elements.

The finger search finds a shortest path that connects the start and end nodes through internal nodes of the tree. This feature guarantees the optimality of the summation algorithm in terms of both space and time efficiency. It avoids the unnecessary computation of the sum of values before a given range and provides the sum of only consecutive values specified by the limits of the summation (see Figure 4.5). The shortest path implies that this algorithm performs the minimum number of operations and supports the most efficient computation of the sum. With the constant time addition, the running time of the summation using the finger search algorithm is logarithmic in the number of the specified consecutive elements, whereas for the fast partial sum algorithm this time is logarithmic in the total number of elements in a sequence.

The fast summation algorithm based on finger search provides basically the same accuracy of the result as the standard sequential summation, since it does not sum up values before the lower limit and processes all of the consecutive values in the same sequential order.

By skipping elements before a given range, this algorithm avoids the issues associated with huge values of temporary sums and significantly reduces the risk of numerical errors. In this aspect, it is more effective compared to computing the sum of consecutive values using the fast partial sum algorithm. A better quality result provides summation from smallest to largest values. However, this method is quite costly. It requires pre-processing, such as sorting all of the values involved, which takes linearithmic time ($O(N \log N)$).

As it was discussed in Chapter 3, it is not always possible to take advantage of theoretically better running time of the finger search algorithm in the efficient representation of a sequence. However, the fast summation algorithm based on finger search addresses the serious issues of the fast partial sum algorithm. The advantage of better accuracy is the main reason why this algorithm is superior to the fast partial sum algorithm in practical applications for computing the sum of arbitrary consecutive elements.

Note also that there is the following difference between the summation and rank algorithms. The path of a summation algorithm can be shorter than the path of its matching rank algorithm. Each rank algorithm terminates search at a node of the deepest level. A fast summation algorithm can terminate computations at an internal node as soon as the specified number of elements has been processed. Such a difference is not significant for B+-trees with large branching factors.

4.3 GEOMETRIC INTERPRETATION

One of the advantages of the augmented level linked B+-trees is that they provide a particularly simple geometric interpretation of the fast summation algorithms that we have considered (see Figure 4.4 and Figure

4.5). The simplifying assumption of this interpretation is that each value in a given sequence is positive.

In terms of the geometric model, a horizontal link between two nodes represents a line segment with the length equal to the value stored in the left node. Therefore, a linked list corresponds to a one-dimensional polygonal chain or a polyline. The sum of consecutive values is equal to the length of a matching polyline. The vertical child-parent links are not involved in the computation of a sum, since their projections on the horizontal dimension do not have lengths. The vertical links are responsible for the connectivity of nodes at different levels.

The relationships between a parent node and its children in the level linked B+-trees can be viewed as a partition of the parent line segment into a polyline of its child line segments. As an algorithm moves up the tree, one horizontal segment covers a sharply increasing number of consecutive segments at the deepest level. In terms of original data, the length of one segment at a high level of the tree provides the sum of a large number of consecutive values of a given sequence.

The summation operations and traversal of a level linked B+-tree follow the simple rules. The traversal of a horizontal link from left to right is equivalent to the addition of a value. The traversal of a horizontal link from right to left is equivalent to the subtraction of a value. The traversal of a vertical link makes no contribution to an accumulated sum.

The performance of a summation algorithm depends on its path in an augmented level linked B+-tree: the smaller number of links in a path, the better performance of a summation algorithm. To avoid confusion, we need to recall the definition of a path in data structures. It is relevant to note that the length of a search path or a computational path is measured in the number of links. It has nothing to do with the distance function in the data space (the space of a given dataset) and thus the length of a matching polyline.

In terms of the geometric interpretation, a computational path in a level linked B+-tree corresponds to a polyline that has both horizontal and vertical segments. As mentioned above, the result of a summation algorithm is determined by the horizontal segments only. The sum of consecutive values in a sequence is equal to the length of a line segment between two points defined by the first and last values. This line segment, as a single geometric object, provides a constant-time computation of the sum, which is, in theory, the best possible performance.

In the general case, there are many ways to partition a given segment into a sequence of smaller segments and to connect end points of the given segment by a polyline. The running time of the computation of the total length is proportional to the number of segments in the polyline. Therefore, there are many ways to achieve the same result, but the running time will vary widely.

A level linked B+-tree, as a geometric data structure, offers time and space efficient facilities to partition and merge line segments associated with values of a given dataset. A summation algorithm on this data structure achieves the optimal performance by finding a polyline with the minimal number of horizontal line segments that cover a matching polyline at the deepest level with a potentially large number of segments.

For convenience of illustration, the diagrams in this chapter show B+-trees with small branching factors. The traversal of vertical links in such trees makes a noticeable contribution to the running time of a summation algorithm based on a shortest path. In practice, the issue of the traversal of vertical links is not significant. To achieve best performance, we choose much larger values of the branching factor. A shortest path in such a B+-tree has a relatively small number of vertical links.

4.4 PARALLEL SUMMATION

It is well known that one problem can be solved by using different methods. The parallel summation is the alternative algorithm that offers fast computation of the sum of the values in a given dataset. The algorithm has interesting properties for comparison with the fast sequential summation supported by augmented B+-trees. The brief discussion of this algorithm is helpful for better understanding of the design principles of efficient algorithms.

Significant progress in computer hardware is one of the key factors of flourishing various parallel algorithms. However, despite the fact that the number of processors in modern systems constantly increases, most computers have relatively small number of processors against a typical size of a user dataset. The running time of parallel summation on such computers is linear, with optimal improvement over the standard sequential summation proportional to the number of processors. This is quite reasonable performance gain for many practical applications, but in processing of large datasets we are interested in logarithmic running time or better. This is why, we consider the ideal machine that provides sufficient number of processors for any given dataset.

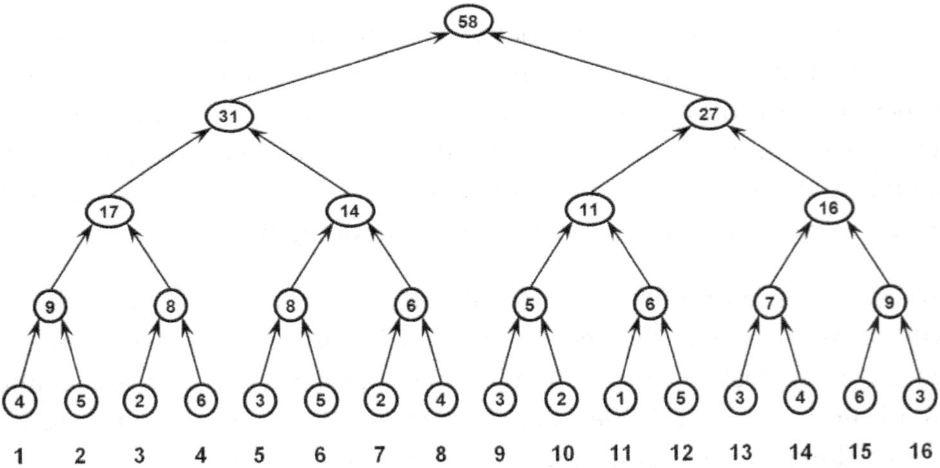

Figure 4.6: A diagram of a parallel summation algorithm for 16 elements. The algorithm takes 4 time steps and performs 15 additions.

The idea of the parallel summation algorithm, which computes the total sum in required logarithmic time, is illustrated in Figure 4.6. The algorithm uses system processors to divide a given dataset into pairs of consecutive elements. The sums of all of the pairs are computed simultaneously and become elements of a new intermediate dataset to be processed at the next stage of the computations. Each stage of processing decreases the number of elements and processors involved by a factor of 2. At the last stage the intermediate dataset contains two elements only. The sum of values of these two elements provides the final result: the total sum of all of the values in the given dataset. The running time of this algorithm is guaranteed to be logarithmic. It is determined by the number of stages, which is logarithmic in the number of elements.

Figure 4.6 shows the diagram of the dynamics of parallel computations as a directed acyclic graph. The shape of this graph has remarkable similarity with a perfect binary tree. In this graph, directed edges represent dependencies between values of sums at consecutive stages. In a perfect binary tree, child-parent links (undirected edges) represent structural relationships between nodes. It means that the graph can be converted into a perfect binary tree with the same values of computed sums if we replace the dependencies with the structural relationships.

This consideration suggests that fast summation algorithms can be developed using binary trees. This is a good practical option, but not the only one. There are several other data structures suitable for this purpose. Moreover, for the choice of the optimal data structure the variety of candidates should be as wide as possible.

Despite the potential of binary and other types of trees, augmented B+-trees offer a number of significant advantages for developing efficient algorithms. In the context of the comparison with parallel summation, they have the attractive property that their structure is globally balanced. Because of this property, the diagrams of the parallel summation algorithm and an augmented B+-tree have close visual resemblance. A dataset of sum values stored at one level of an augmented B+ tree (see Figure 4.2) mirrors a dataset computed at one stage of the parallel summation algorithm (see Figure 4.6). The difference between these two datasets is in the number of data elements that contribute to a sum value. In the parallel algorithm, the value is the sum of two predecessor values. In a B+-tree, the value is the sum of values of all children of one parent.

The obvious drawback of the parallel summation algorithm is the loss of intermediate results. It is designed to compute only one value of the total sum of all of the values in a given dataset. Except for the final sum value and the given dataset, the results of all of the other stages are not saved. If a user modifies just one element in the original dataset, the computation of a new sum involves costly re-computation of all of the intermediate results.

However, most of these re-computations are unnecessary, since many intermediate results remain unchanged due to fixed dependencies between results of consecutive stages. This fact implies that the parallel algorithm does not have the ability to re-use valid intermediate results in subsequent computations.

The augmented trees are designed to address this performance issue by storing any relevant pre-computed data in internal nodes and providing efficient modifying operations. These data are used in subsequent processing to avoid useless re-computation and to minimize the number of operations to compute a result or answer a query.

The important aspect of the parallel summation algorithm is that its logarithmic running time is achieved by high computational cost and, thus, high energy consumption. The total number of operations performed by the parallel algorithm is linear. It is at least the same as for the standard sequential algorithm. The fast sequential summation algorithms using an augmented B+-tree provide the solution to this problem. These algorithms guarantee both logarithmic running time and logarithmic number of operations.

The factor that limits the use of parallel summation algorithms is the high cost of computer hardware. Processors are orders of magnitude more expensive than memory elements. In addition, a system with a fixed number of processors does not provide general scale independent solution for parallel summation. The important practical advantage of the fast sequential summation algorithms on augmented B+-trees is that they do not need supercomputers and can run on the cheapest single processor systems. The main system restriction is imposed by the amount of available memory.

To summarize, the parallel summation algorithm is fast and important for many applications, but this is not the best example of effective use of computers.

4.5 SUMMARY

The fast summation algorithms are of fundamental importance in numerous application areas of business and science. When the standard sequential summation algorithm becomes a bottleneck in processing of large datasets, it should be replaced with a more efficient algorithm. The popular method based on an array of pre-computed partial sums has serious limitations, such as a small set of efficient primary operations provided by the array and the accuracy issue for arbitrary ranges of consecutive values.

The optimal choice for a complex algorithm is a balanced tree. The augmented level linked B+-trees are particularly attractive for this purpose. In addition to a wide range of efficient primary operations, they offer two types of summation algorithms, which guarantee both logarithmic running time and logarithmic total number of operations. Because of this performance, they are superior not only to sequential algorithms on basic data structures but also to parallel algorithms. Their accuracy of numerical computations is practically the same as that of the standard sequential summation, which is important for large scale applications.

One of the main design methods that helped us to develop the new efficient algorithms is the method of augmenting a data structure. At first, we applied this method to obtain a level linked B+-tree that stores counts of sequence elements and, thus, supports an efficient representation of a sequence. Unlike search trees, its fast rank algorithm uses not only efficient search but also efficient summation of counts. We tried to exploit this feature to obtain a fast summation algorithm. However, the straightforward replacement of counts with sums of sequence values, does not work because a resulting linked data structure without counts no longer provides efficient sequence facilities.

An augmented level linked B+-tree that supports fast summation algorithms stores two accumulated datasets that look similar but serve different purposes. The counts of sequence elements are associated only with the structural invariants of the tree, whereas the sums are associated with both the structural invariants and the values of a given dataset. Such an advanced data structure is obtained by augmenting an efficient representation of a sequence, which inserts into nodes a new dataset of the sums of sequence values synchronized with the counts of the values.

We introduced the fast sequential summation algorithms through the search for a shortest path between start and end nodes of a linked data structure. A fast summation algorithm of this kind represents a shortest path algorithm that accumulates values of pre-computed sums in visited nodes. At the same time, the geometric interpretation of these algorithms suggests that there might be another way to obtain the same summation results. In particular, the set of horizontal links detected by the finger search algorithm can also be detected by the top-down algorithm that applies containment and intersection operations to the ranges matching links in a level linked B+-tree. Such an alternative algorithm is used in aggregation trees (see Chapter 5).

The advantage of our approach is that the shortest path algorithms are sequential algorithms. For this reason, the new fast summation algorithms are closely related to the standard sequential summation. The algorithms for the computations of a partial sum and a sum of arbitrary consecutive values represent enhanced variants of the standard sequential summation algorithm.

Chapter 5: Semigroup

Our current variant of augmented level linked B+-trees provides a wide range of efficient algorithms for representations of sets and sequences both ordered and unordered. It offers efficient random access to data elements, search, insertion and deletion. In addition, this tree provides fast summation algorithms. All of the primary algorithms take logarithmic time in the worst case. This performance makes our data structure attractive for the analysis of large datasets. For example, with these facilities we can compute in logarithmic time the mean of any consecutive values, which is one of the fundamental statistical characteristics of data.

The minimum and maximum values in a given range are the other important characteristics of the data distribution frequently required in practical applications. Thus, it is desirable to add efficient facilities to answer such queries. As before, linear running time is not acceptable for processing of large datasets. The new algorithms must have the efficiency compatible with that of fast summation algorithms on augmented B+-trees. The performance is expected to be logarithmic or better.

When a range is specified in the key space, the problem is reduced to the queries that provide the number and/or all of the elements in the range. In relatively simple applications, such problems are efficiently solved with balanced search trees and ordered arrays. The task of finding the minimum or maximum value in a given range is trivial for ordered data. However, these basic data structures do not offer a wide variety of efficient operations for complex applications.

Here, we focus on the problem for a range of consecutive elements without any assumption of the order of given data. In addition, the input may contain duplicate values. Thus, we choose efficient sequences instead of sets to store the user data. A range in a sequence is specified by the ranks of the first and last elements.

This problem is more challenging, since for unordered data the basic data structures support only sequential search, which is not acceptable for large datasets due to its linear running time. Pre-processing a given range, such as sorting elements, or creating an auxiliary data structure that provides a fast algorithm cannot be used either. Such methods add at least linear time in the size of the range.

The data structures that provide the required efficient algorithms on ranges should offer the construction methods before their new algorithms can be used by a client. In addition, these data structures may implement operations to save modifications to user and internal data. These restrictions imply that we need to develop the general purpose algorithms similar to fast summation that can be applied to both ordered and unordered data.

In this chapter, we approach this problem using the mathematical concept of a semigroup and the generalization capacity of augmented data structures. The idea of the solution is to extend facilities of our sequences to implement the new level of abstraction. The efficient representation of a semigroup using augmented level linked B+-trees is an instructive example of achieving generality without loss of efficiency. It demonstrates the great potential of advanced data structures and modern programming techniques for solving important practical problems. This example is interesting from both design and implementation perspectives.

5.1 DEFINITION AND LIMITATIONS

In mathematics, a semigroup is defined as a set with an associative binary operation on elements of the set. By the definition, a semigroup is almost a set, which is why it is a fundamental and highly abstract mathematical concept. Its level of generality is only a bit lower than that of a set.

Despite the simple and abstract definition, the concept of a semigroup is effective in practical applications. Its power follows from the fact that it unifies various types of binary operations, including such unrelated as the addition and the selection of the minimum value. This property of a semigroup is of particular interest to us in the context of developing the required algorithms for the efficient computation of statistical characteristics of large datasets. This is the main application area of a semigroup that we consider in this chapter.

In the general case, the representation of a semigroup is achieved if a sequence supports an associative binary operation on its elements. For this reason, the programming implementation of a semigroup using a basic data structure, such as a linked list or an array, is a straightforward task. To answer a range query, a binary operation is applied in sequential order to all of the elements of a given range. The computations using the binary operation accumulate or update one result value. Unlike advanced data structures, there is no additional internal complexity. A basic data structure stores only elements of a user dataset.

A semigroup based on a basic data structure helps us to promote the clarity of a conceptual solution and its implementation code through the use of high level mathematical abstractions. Nevertheless, it is too slow for large datasets.

The solution to the performance problems of basic data structures is to replace them with advanced data structures that provide a wider variety of efficient operations. As we have already seen from the development of sequences, achieving the high efficiency of a representation based on an advanced data structure faces a number of challenges. The performance comes at the cost of the increased complexity of a data structure with all of its consequences. And the implementation of a semigroup imposes specific constraints.

The main complication for the development of the representation follows from the fact that a semigroup is defined by one binary operation only. This feature affects the complexity of implementation and to some degree the overall performance of advanced data structures. This is a serious limitation, because their primary algorithms use pre-computed values stored in internal nodes.

The wider variety of operations enables the development of simpler and more efficient algorithms. In terms of performance, we have already discussed an example of the benefit of the inverse operation. Given an array of pre-computed partial sums, the sum of values in any range can be obtained in constant time using the subtraction, which the inverse of the addition. For comparison, sequential processing of each value in the range takes linear time.

There is a similar situation in the implementation of primary algorithms on augmented B+-trees. The pre-computed value in a parent node is the result of a binary operation applied to all of its children. The insert a child operation is supported by the addition. There is no need for another operation to update the parent value. The delete operation, however, is the most efficient if we subtract the child value from the parent value.

Without the inverse operation, the implementation of the delete operation is a bit different. It recomputes the sum of all children and saves the result in the parent node. This is the same method as we use in the bottom-up construction algorithm. The performance of this update algorithm is a bit worse. Nevertheless, it takes constant time, since the number of children does not exceed the maximum size. Normally, such a difference in performance is not significant.

Using an inverse operation might be possible at the implementation level, but this is a sub-optimal approach to achieving a unified programming solution. There is the important difference between the addition and the minimum of two values. For the addition, there is the inverse operation, which is not allowed in theory but can be used in practice at the implementation level to improve performance of internal algorithms. The minimum and maximum of two values do not have inverse operations in principle.

The algorithms specific to particular binary operations increase the complexity of the implementation code. Although this approach is acceptable for performance optimization, it should be avoided in the implementation of the general purpose advanced data structures and algorithms. It is better not to assume that an inversion operation exists. In this chapter, we show how to use one data structure and one algorithm to support several different range queries for different types of binary operations.

5.2 ADDITIVE SEMIGROUP

The current variant of augmented level linked B+-trees offers a wide variety of operations for the efficient representation of sequences plus two summation algorithms that break the linear running time barrier. Since the addition is an associative binary operation, these data structures have the potential to replace basic data structures in applications using additive semigroups. It only remains to verify that these fast summation algorithms meet the requirements for a semigroup.

The fast partial sum algorithm supports the efficient computation of the sum of all values in a given range. However, its application involves not only the addition but also the subtraction (see Section 4.2). For this reason, this summation algorithm does not meet the formal requirements for the additive semigroup.

The second efficient algorithm provides the same sum using only the addition of values stored in visited nodes and does not need any other operation to obtain the result. This fact means that the summation algorithm based on finger search satisfies the formal requirements for the additive semigroup. It also means that we achieve the required efficient representation of an additive semigroup with one fast summation algorithm only. In theory, it is suitable for any computer type that supports the addition.

The efficient representation of an additive semigroup is the extension of the efficient sequence, which provides the fast summation algorithm for any given range. However, what we achieved is not yet a general purpose computer representation of a semigroup, since it supports only one type of a binary operation. Our main objective is to devise the general purpose representation, which works for any associative binary operation with the best possible efficiency.

The idea that helps us to solve this problem follows from the feature of the finger search summation algorithm that it computes the sum of arbitrary consecutive values using only one type of a binary operation. This is not only the advantage of the implementation simplicity over the partial sum algorithm. It also suggests that the finger search algorithm has the potential to support fast computation of characteristics of a dataset using different types of binary operations. Below, we will exploit this idea to achieve the generalized computer representation of a mathematical semigroup.

5.3 SEMIGROUP WITH MINIMUM OF TWO VALUES

In order to better understand why the finger search algorithm can help us to find the solution for the required general purpose representation, we will consider another example of a semigroup with a different type of a binary operation: the minimum of two values. The implementation of this variant is a good test for our approach, since unlike the addition this binary operation does not have the inverse operation. This representation of a semigroup will provide all of the efficient facilities of a sequence plus the fast computation of the minimum value in a given range.

The similarity of binary operations unified by the concept of a semigroup suggests that many algorithms for the new variant of a semigroup can be adapted from those for the additive semigroup. This can be achieved by simple replacing the addition with the minimum of two values. For the highest level of the generality, the type of a binary operation should be the only difference between two variants of a semigroup in all of the matching primary algorithms.

As with any other advanced data structure, before the first use we must build the new augmented level linked B+-tree. We start with the data structure of minimum values. The task can be completed by using the properly adapted bottom-up construction algorithm.

The data structure shown in Figure 5.1 is built with the binary operation that selects the minimum of two values. The distinctive feature of this data structure is the heap order: the value in a parent node is the minimum of all of the values stored in its child nodes. This variant of a level linked B+-tree provides the same facilities as a binary heap based on a complete binary tree. The heap ordered property enables this data structure to support efficient operations of a priority queue on the whole dataset. This is a very useful property but not sufficient, since our current task is to extend the efficient facilities for range queries by developing the fast algorithm that finds the minimum value in any given range of consecutive elements.

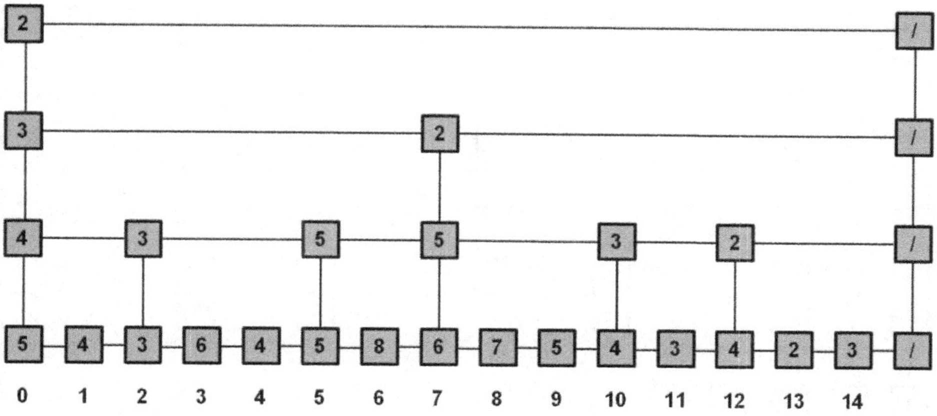

Figure 5.1: A level linked B+-tree of minimum values of consecutive elements in a given sequence, which is stored at the deepest level of the tree. Each value in an internal node is the result of the binary operation on the sub-tree rooted at the node.

In this context, we face the same problem as for the data structure of sums (see Figure 4.2). The data structure of minimum values stores in internal nodes useful pre-computed data. However, it does not have the ability to efficiently support the range queries, because it is a slow sequence. It provides the efficiency of a linked list.

This time the problem should not be too challenging, since we can apply the same method that was used to develop fast summation algorithms. The efficient sequence facilities are supported by the counts of elements. They must be stored in internal nodes of the tree together with the minimum values. The new data structure is the combination of two data structures of minimum values and counts of elements (see Figure 5.2).

This data structure provides the desired efficient facilities of a sequence: random access to data, the identification of elements by ranks and the navigation through internal nodes to select proper minimum values of sub-trees. It means that the data structure is prepared for the implementation of the algorithm, which finds or computes the minimum value in any given range. In the general case, the algorithm starts and terminates at any two nodes of the deepest level that contain the first and last values of a given range.

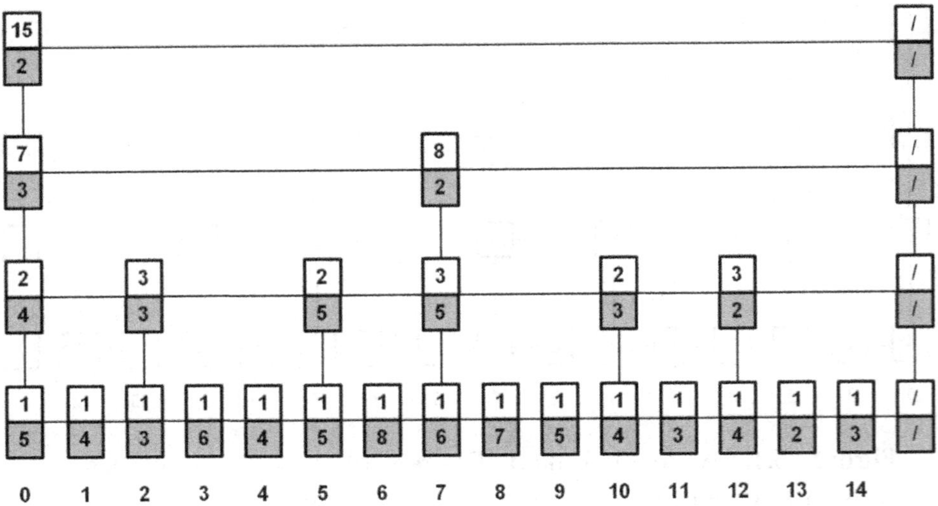

Figure 5.2: A level linked B+-tree that computes the minimum of arbitrary consecutive values in logarithmic time. Each internal node stores both a count and a minimum of consecutive values of a given sequence.

The performance of this algorithm is determined by the length of its search and computational path. In terms of the optimality, there is no better choice than the shortest path, which is detected by the finger search algorithm. This is why, the algorithm of the fast computation of the minimum value in a given range uses the same path as the fast summation algorithm (see Figure 4.5). The only difference is that instead of the addition it uses the binary operation, which selects the minimum of two values.

The new variant of an augmented level linked B+-tree provides the required extension of efficient facilities of a sequence for range queries. At the same time, it offers the substantially wider variety of operations than a priority queue, because it supports the efficient representation of a sequence. In particular, a user can insert and delete values anywhere within a sequence or a given range. These operations maintain both the relative order of elements at the deepest level and the heap order in internal nodes.

5.4 SEMIGROUP WITH MAXIMUM OF TWO VALUES

The representation of a semigroup with the maximum of two values is almost identical to that with the minimum of two values. Its implementation is a trivial task of replacing the type of the binary operation in the previous variant of a semigroup. The new augmented data structure supports an efficient sequence and the fast computation of the maximum value in a given range of a sequence (see Figure 5.3). Due to the optimality of the shortest path, the fast algorithm for the maximum value in a range uses the same path as for the minimum value and the computation of the sum.

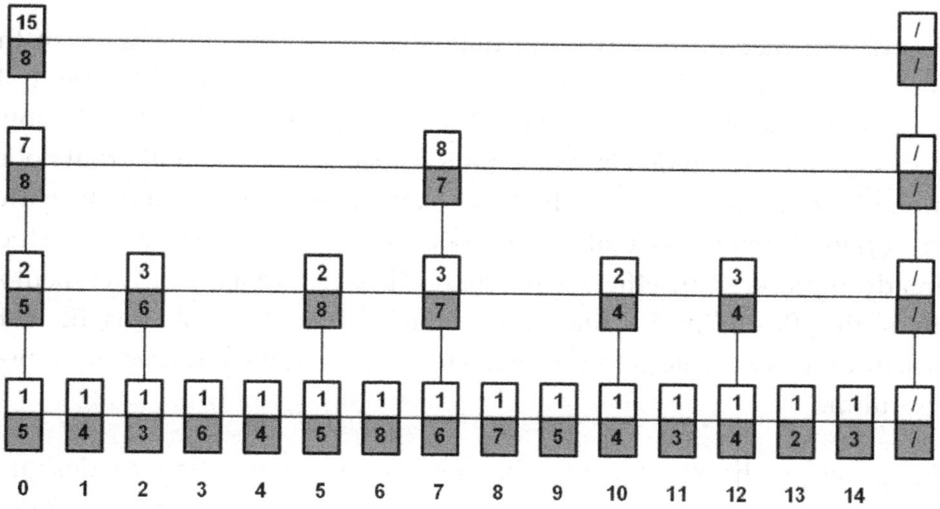

Figure 5.3: A level linked B+-tree that computes the maximum of arbitrary consecutive values in logarithmic time. Each internal node stores both a count and a maximum of consecutive values of a given sequence.

5.5 COMPLEX SEMIGROUP

The new extensions allow us to efficiently compute a number of important characteristics of a data distribution in any given range or the whole sequence: the sum, the mean, the minimum and the maximum. Given this variety of efficient algorithms for the computation of specific characteristics, the next related question is: what is the most effective way of using them in practice?

In most applications, we need to know more than one characteristic of a data distribution. The simple and obvious method is to construct as many semigroups based on augmented B+-trees as needed. Within this approach, a user algorithm creates for one user dataset several augmented B+-trees, each prepared for one specific binary operation. This method has two serious drawbacks: the loss of space due to storing the same user dataset in several data structures and the complexity of synchronization of operations on different data structures. These issues can be addressed by another method, which we consider below.

This design method of advanced data structures takes advantage of the storage facilities of B+-trees that support space efficient multiple augmenting (see Section 3.7). The strength of this method is that it allows us to store more than one implementation specific dataset in internal nodes of one B+-tree. Using this method, we can combine several sub-structures for different binary operations in one complex data structure, which already represents an efficient sequence. It is important that this method offers the flexibility in fine-tuning the combination of specific sub-structures to compute several characteristics of data required in a user algorithm.

The general scheme of using the method of augmenting to design a complex data structure that supports several efficient algorithms required in a user application can be outlined as follows.

The first task is to achieve the efficient representation of a mathematical sequence. As an underlying data structure, a level linked B+-tree provides a number of useful fast operations to find, insert and delete elements. The elements of a given dataset are stored in nodes of the deepest linked list, which is a slow sequence with respect to random access. This is why, we build the sub-structure of counts of the nodes, which store elements of the given dataset (in short, counts of elements), by saving these counts in internal nodes of the B+-tree. The counts of elements are structural invariants. They are independent of the values stored at the deepest level, implementation specific data to be inserted into internal nodes and the type of a binary operation. The sub-structure of counts supports efficient search algorithms that guarantee fast random access to the data elements and fast access to implementation data in internal nodes of the B+-tree. Finger search finds a shortest path between any two given nodes of the deepest level. As we will see later, this algorithm is crucial to the development of a semigroup. Due to the importance of these sequence facilities, the sub-structure of counts of elements is implemented by each variant of an augmented B+ tree. In terms of the method of augmenting, such a B+-tree implements single augmenting with counts of elements.

The second task is to build and add internal sub-structures and datasets for binary operations specified by a user. Within the unified semigroup model, this task is relatively simple. Given a user dataset at the deepest level, each augmenting uses a binary operation to build a new sub-structure with the specific dataset stored in internal nodes of the level linked B+-tree. Note that unlike the sub-structure of counts of elements, the new accumulated values in the internal nodes depend on both the values of the user dataset and the binary operation. The method of augmenting is applied as many times as needed to the same data structure in order to implement all of the efficient algorithms required in a user application. Such iterative multiple augmenting can be regarded as a method of building several data structures within one.

In Figure 5.4, we illustrate this method of multiple augmenting with the complex data structures, which efficiently computes all of the discussed characteristics of a data distribution. Each internal node of this B+-tree is augmented with the minimum, maximum and sum values computed for a sub-tree rooted at the internal node. The counts of elements in the internal nodes are not associated with binary operations. They support efficient sequence and navigation facilities.

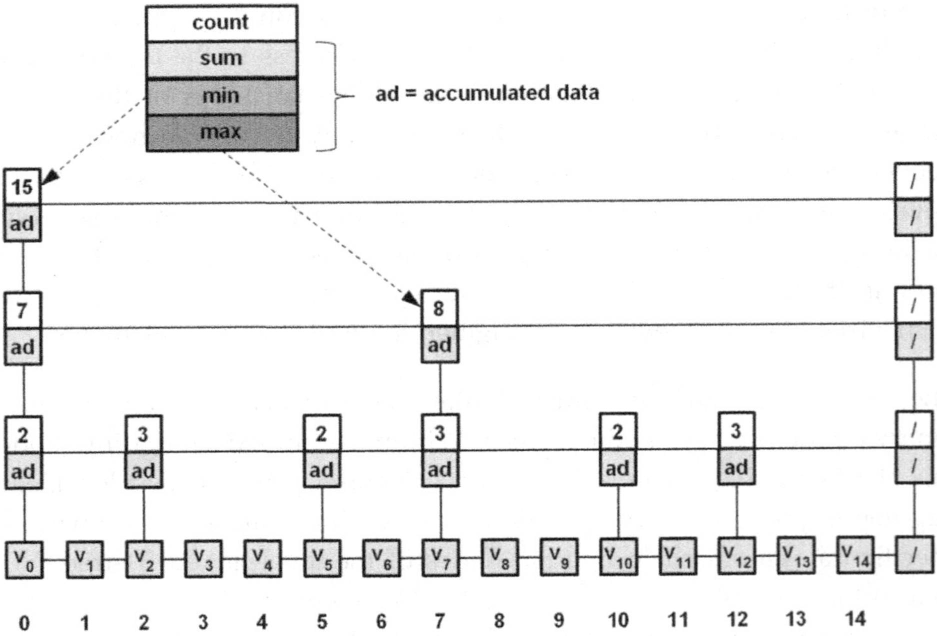

Figure 5.4: A level linked B+-tree obtained by multiple augmenting. The nodes of the deepest level store values of a given sequence. The data stored in internal nodes support efficient computation of the following characteristics of arbitrary consecutive values: the minimum, the maximum, the sum and the mean.

5.5.1 Role of Finger Search

The role of the finger search algorithm in the representation of a semigroup using an augmented level linked B+-tree deserves a more detailed explanation. As we have already seen, the only difference between fast computations of the sum and the minimum of values in a range is the type of a binary operation. The main similarity is that both of these fast algorithms use the same path provided by finger search. Moreover, all of the fast algorithms computing specific characteristics of a data distribution in a given range use the same shortest path. It is obvious that a computational algorithm using a shortest path is the most efficient: it performs the minimum number of binary operations on data stored in the nodes on the path. It is also important to note that the same result can be obtained by using different paths. For example, the standard sequential algorithm that visits each node of a linked list is also based on the shortest path between start and end nodes. However, in a level linked B+-tree this is not normally the best choice, since a path between two distant nodes of the deepest level is shorter through internal nodes than through nodes of the deepest level (see Figure 5.5).

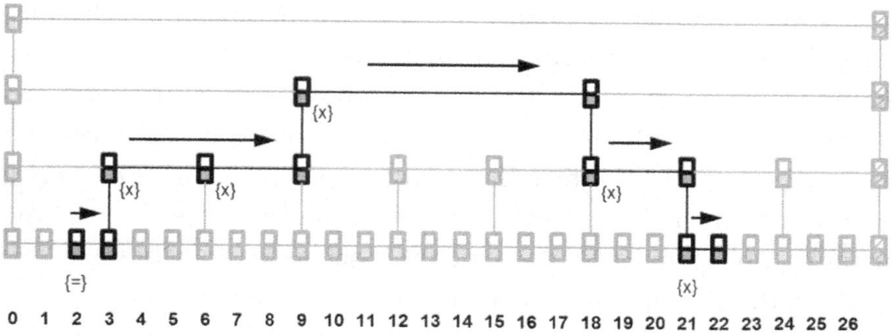

Figure 5.5: Illustration of the efficient computation of several characteristics of a given dataset using the shortest path in a level linked B+-tree detected by finger search. The symbol {x} denotes a binary operation on complex data (see Figure 5.4). This computational algorithm supersedes the fast summation algorithm shown in Figure 4.5.

Each of the fast algorithms using the shortest path through internal nodes not only delivers the same result as sequential processing of each value at the deepest level, but also preserves the order of slow sequential processing. The last feature is essential for the correctness of the computations with an associative binary operation. There is no such restriction on a commutative binary operation. In a level linked B+-tree, the shortest path, which is re-used by several algorithms, offers the same level of the generality for client algorithms as a chain of nodes in a linked list. For these reasons, computational processing using the finger search algorithm plays the same role as sequential processing in a linked list. It can be regarded as a fast variant of the standard sequential processing on linear data structures.

5.5.2 Advantage of Multiple Augmenting

When a software library does not offer advanced data structures, the typical approach to complex problems is to develop a solution based on several relatively simple data structures with different efficiency of primary operations. The main problem with this kind of solutions is that one inefficient operation can lead to significant loss of the overall performance. Another problem is that such custom solutions are notoriously difficult to improve. In this situation, the method of multiple augmenting is one of the first to be considered to fix such performance problems. The new solution ideally uses one advanced data structure that offers a wide variety of efficient operations. If a specific operation is too slow, augmenting helps us to improve its performance. The method of augmenting an advanced data structure enables us to achieve a solution without inefficient operations. Thus, there is no need to worry about frequencies of specific operations. And there is no need for adding to the solution another data structure, which may fix the performance of one primary operation but has another slow operation required in a user algorithm.

The important advantage of the method of multiple augmenting is that it avoids the construction and use of additional data structures that offer only a sub-set of efficient operations required in a user application. One advanced data structure supports all of the efficient operations required in a user algorithm. Thus, multiple augmenting addresses the issue of the synchronization of operations on several different data structures. In an augmented data structure, different types of datasets are synchronized through the same connectivity of nodes of an underlying data structure. Quite obviously, this benefit comes at the price of the internal complexity of advanced data structures, but it remains hidden from users of fast algorithms.

5.6 AGGREGATION TREES

The main focus of this book is on level linked B+-trees, which are stored in internal memory of a computer system. The structure of these trees is different from that of classical balanced trees that do not connect sibling nodes. Despite the different structure, the classical trees also have the capability to efficiently compute the key statistical characteristics of a dataset. Here, we limit the scope of the discussion to B+-trees that store and efficiently process huge datasets in external memory. These trees are the main data structures used in the largest scale applications. Note that for this discussion the structure of trees is more important than the type of storage. The interesting aspect of this comparison is that the same results can be obtained by applying different types of algorithms.

SQL provides aggregate functions that can be used for the fast computation of the statistical characteristics: ***min, max, sum, count, avg***. These queries are supported by the aggregation tree, which represents a variant of an augmented B+-tree similar to those discussed here. In a B+-tree for external searching, objects are identified by their keys. For the best performance of operations on ranges, such a B+-tree stores objects in non-decreasing order of their keys. An augmented tree of this type implements the sub-structure of counts for efficient computing order statistics, but the tree is not designed to represent an unordered sequence.

Each B+-tree has the structure optimized for sequential access to elements of a user dataset stored at the deepest level. However, a B+-tree for external searching does not guarantee that all of the sibling nodes at each internal level are linked or are adjacent to each other in storage pages. For this reason, this type of B+-trees does not support the shortest path algorithm similar to finger search and we need another approach.

The algorithm that efficiently computes statistical characteristics of a dataset in a given range is based on the top-down search for the minimum number of nodes of an aggregation B+-tree, which are fully covered by the given range. If a node is partially covered, we test all of its children. The typical implementation of this algorithm is recursive. The search starts from the root and normally passes through all of the levels of the B+-tree.

The augmented level linked B+-trees also support the efficient top-down range query algorithm. It finds the same nodes as finger search. However, the order the nodes found is implementation specific. This is not a problem for commutative binary operations, but might be a problem for associative binary operations.

Another potential issue is that such an algorithm in theory is not asymptotically optimal for this type of B+-trees. A top-down algorithm visits all of the levels of a B+-tree and, thus, its running time is logarithmic in the total number of user data elements in the tree. The running time of the shortest path algorithm using finger search is logarithmic in the number of elements in a given range, since it visits only as many low levels of the tree as needed. As we already mentioned, this superiority of finger search is rather theoretical than practical. The high performance of algorithms based on the top-down search is sufficient for a wide variety of practical applications.

The top-down variants of computational algorithms offer a number of advantages important for practical applications. They effectively exploit the vertical dimension of a tree and do not require that the tree be level linked. These algorithms work on all types of balanced trees, including multi-dimensional. In a broader context, the top-down variants of computational algorithms are more general than algorithms using finger search. However, for the efficient representation of a semigroup the suitability of a top-down algorithm is determined by the order of nodes found by the algorithm. The degree of the generalization by binary operations, which can be achieved in a semigroup, depends on whether the order of nodes is consistent with an associative binary operation or not.

5.7 STANDARD DEVIATION

The standard deviation is another essential statistical characteristic of data, which is frequently used in numerous application areas. The current variant of augmented level linked B+-trees guarantees only linear running time of the computation of this characteristic. This is a potential performance bottleneck for large scale applications. If we achieve the same logarithmic running time as for the mean of consecutive values, this would provide a substantial performance gain in practical applications of our representation of a semigroup.

The standard deviation can be computed by taking the square root of the variance

$$\left(\frac{1}{n-m}\sum_{i=m}^{n-1} a_i^2\right) - \left(\frac{1}{n-m}\sum_{i=m}^{n-1} a_i\right)^2$$

The fast computation of the standard deviation based on this method is not directly covered by our representation of a semigroup, since it uses more than one operation, including the subtraction, which the inverse of the addition.

All of the operations in this method take constant time, except for the computations of two sums for the variance: the sum of values and the sum of squared values. We have already developed fast summation algorithms, but the current variant of augmented level linked B+-tree does not yet support fast summation of squared values of elements in a given range.

This task can be accomplished with an additional augmented B+-tree. But, as discussed before, this is not an effective approach. It would be much more practical to take advantage of multiple augmenting and implement the new efficient algorithm as an extension to the data structure that already supports fast summation. For this purpose, we add to each internal node the new type of implementation data: the sum of squared values of the sub-tree rooted at the node. As a result of this augmenting, one internal node stores the following data: the count of elements, the sum of values, the sum of squared values, the minimum and maximum values.

This approach enables the computation of the standard deviation simultaneously with the mean of consecutive values and other characteristics of data. The logarithmic performance is guaranteed by the finger search algorithm, which provides the shortest path for computing each characteristic required in a user application. Table 5.1 summarizes the computational complexities of primary operations, including the extensions offered by the efficient representation of a semigroup.

	Linked List	Array	Augmented B+-Tree
Insertion	$O(1)$	$O(N)$	$O(\log N)$
Deletion	$O(1)$	$O(N)$	$O(\log N)$
Rank	$O(R)$	$O(1)$	$O(\log N)$
Sum	$O(K)$	$O(K)$	$O(\log K)$
Min	$O(K)$	$O(K)$	$O(\log K)$
Max	$O(K)$	$O(K)$	$O(\log K)$
Mean	$O(K)$	$O(K)$	$O(\log K)$
Deviation	$O(K)$	$O(K)$	$O(\log K)$

Table 5.1: The computational complexities of primary operations of unordered sequences based on basic data structures and an augmented B+-tree that supports a semigroup. N is the number of elements in a given dataset. K is the number of elements in a range. Rank - retrieve an element at a given rank R.

The current variant of an augmented level linked B+-tree supports the general purpose representation of a semigroup, which works for any number of binary operations. It can efficiently compute several important characteristics of a data distribution in any given range using the shortest path provided by the finger search algorithm. Multiple augmenting is the design method, which extends the variety of efficient operations provided by one data structure. The representation of a semigroup discussed in this section has been achieved by the extension of the efficient representation of a mathematical sequence.

5.8 TIME AND SPACE EFFICIENCY

A semigroup is a high level abstraction designed to cover a wide variety of specific mathematical objects and concepts. As an abstract mathematical concept, it is not concerned with performance aspects, which are important for programming implementations. In applications processing large datasets, the time and space efficiency of operations and data types are the essential parameters that make a representation of a mathematical concept useful in practice. For the most efficient variants, we assume that the computational complexity of an associative binary operation is constant.

We also assume that an element in a node of the deepest level and a precomputed value in an internal node use a constant amount of space.

The application area of the advanced representation of a semigroup can be expanded if we remove the restrictions on a fixed size of a data element and a constant time of a binary operation. In this case, the representation based on an augmented level linked B+-tree can be used for complex objects, such as sets and sequences. The benefits of such variants of semigroups should be measured against the potential loss of space and run time efficiency.

A classic example of such a complex object is a string of characters with the binary operation of concatenation. Since a string has an arbitrary length, it is normally represented by a data structure that uses a variable amount of memory. The space requirement for such a semigroup is quite significant, since in the straightforward implementation an internal node stores a pre-computed string, which copies a large range of a string at the deepest level. For this reason, each level of an augmented B+-tree duplicates all of the user data stored at the deepest level. The overall performance of this semigroup is highly sensitive to the choice of an underlying data structure. In terms of the efficient concatenation, a linked list offers much better performance than an array. But this list operation is not effective if copying is involved in the implementation of a semigroup. In addition, random access to elements in a linked list is slow. A better option is a string based on an advanced data structure that provides a wide variety of operations that take logarithmic time, including the concatenation. However, the issue of copying data to be stored in internal nodes remains important.

5.9 COPY AND REFERENCE SEMANTICS

The modern programming languages support both copy and reference semantics. The common belief is that reference semantics is the best choice to achieve the optimal time and space efficiency in programming solutions. Unfortunately, this is not always true. This approach becomes less and less effective as the complexity of data structures and algorithms increases. In the implementation of advanced data structures, such as augmented level linked B+-trees, this approach is normally avoided because of non-trivial issues of resource management.

In the context of the design and implementation of a semigroup, the differences in the binary operations to be covered by a general purpose representation are particularly important. For the binary operations that select minimum or maximum of two values, it is acceptable to return the result as a reference to an object, since no resource allocation is involved. As for the addition, its implementation details vary quite significantly from one data type to another. The most suitable option is that the operation returns a reference to a new object, since without creating a new object the reference semantics of the addition is quite complex. The result represents a data structure, which is internally similar to an expression tree or a DAG. This option not only increases the overall complexity of the implementation, but also may cause performance issues if the internal structure is unbalanced.

The use of the copy semantics is the preferable approach to the implementation of a general purpose semigroup. It is consistent with the mathematical definitions of this concept and associative binary operations and avoids all of the complications associated with the reference semantics. The loss of performance is not substantial for small size data types and constant time binary operations. The performance gain provided by augmented level linked B+-trees is much more significant. It is achieved through the optimal connectivity and storing pre-computed data in internal nodes.

5.10 MONOID

A monoid is another high level mathematical concept, which is widely used by programmers in solutions to practical problems. The reasons for its popularity are the same as for a semigroup: the simplicity and the power of the high level abstraction. The definition of a monoid equips a set with an associative binary operation and an identity element. As we can see, the only difference from a semigroup is the additional requirement for an identity element. At first glance, it seems that the difference is not significant, since for many types of binary operations, such as the addition and multiplication, the support for an identity element in programming languages has no serious complications. However, the minimum and maximum of two values are different from other binary operations. Their identity elements have infinite values. In the general purpose programming solutions, the representation of infinite numbers is a non-trivial and error-prone task due to problems of portability and type conversions.

The definition of a semigroup does not specify an identity element. This is why, a semigroup offers two important advantages over a monoid. It is a more general mathematical concept, and it is simpler from a programming implementation perspective. Nevertheless, irrespective of the specific choice made, large scale projects gain major benefits of the generality, efficiency, clarity and the optimal cost of development when their solutions to client problems are based on the high level mathematical concepts. It is reasonable to replace the representation of a semigroup or a monoid with specialized algorithms only in performance-critical applications.

5.11 NUMERIC TYPES

The choice of a numeric type is of great practical importance for achieving the high quality of the representation of a semigroup. The decision depends on the type of an associative binary operation. For example, the operations that select minimum or maximum of two values do not cause any complications. If values of given operands are valid, the result is valid too, since it is equal to the value of one of the operands. However, the other types of operations, such the addition and multiplication, may produce a result value, which is out of range of a data type.

The main issues of the addition have been previously discussed in the context of fast summation algorithms, refer to Section 4.2. Integer numbers are preferable choice in terms of the best possible accuracy. For floating-point numbers, numerical errors create another problem specific to the representation of a semigroup. Strictly speaking, floating-point numbers do not satisfy the mathematical requirements for associativity of binary operations. Even in the simple case of three variables, there is no guarantee that the floating-point computation of a sum $(a + b) + c$ will provide exactly the same result as $a + (b + c)$. As the number of values increases, the result of computations becomes less accurate. The numerical errors are responsible for the complication that invariants associated with augmented data in internal nodes of a B+-tree may become invalid. A semigroup using floating-point numbers must control accuracy within limits acceptable for a large scale application. Because of these issues, the demo code in this book does not use floating-point data types.

5.12 GENERIC PROGRAMMING

In modern programming languages, the general purpose representation of a semigroup can be implemented using different techniques. The best choice is generic programming, which in C++ is based on templates. Even the name of this technique suggests that it is designed to support generalizations in programming solutions. The technique offers the highest level of the generality for the representation of abstract concepts (not only mathematical) through parameterized types. A template parameter is an abstraction, which unifies a set of related concrete types both built-in and user defined. A user selects a suitable concrete type for each template parameter in order to build a class or a function required in a specific application. In the context of the development of the general purpose representation of a semigroup, the most important are the types of data elements and the types of function objects representing binary operations.

The main strength of generic programming is that the code, which implements a class template or a function template, is uniform in the sense that this code does not depend on any allowed concrete type. But why the uniformity of the implementation code is important for advanced data structures?

A typical implementation of one concrete advanced data structure, such as a level linked B+-tree, may contain several thousands of lines. Writing such concrete implementations for each possible combination of concrete types of a data element and a binary operation is very costly and quickly leads to the problem of unmanageable complexity. As a result, the generalization capacity of this approach is limited. It is possible to have a number of concrete implementations that cover the main application areas that we know at present. But there is no guarantee that we will be able to respond effectively to challenges that will arise in the future.

The generic programming technique provides nearly perfect solution to these problems: The large and complex implementation code of a template is written once and then is used with a wide variety of concrete types as many times as required. Given a template definition, the code for supplied concrete types is automatically generated by a compiler. Since the cost of the development is constant, it becomes less and less significant factor the longer the software is in use.

In this section, we discuss algorithms useful in practical application from the implementation aspects that may have effect on the generality of the representation. We show how to deal with unrelated binary operations. How to find a unified signature for operations involved. How to reduce different implementation specific code for algorithms to a unified variant. Achieving this makes our template algorithm parameterized on the binary operation. One of the goals of this discussion is to show the difference in template implementations between basic and advanced data structures.

5.12.1 Basic Data Structures

Since we would like to illustrate the main ideas, we avoid technicalities of templates by using concrete types and relatively simple variants of algorithms on basic data structures, such as arrays. For the same reason, instead of function objects for the representation of binary operations in the demo code we use functions.

We start with operator-based variants of algorithms. The code below shows the fragment of a typical implementation that finds the minimum value in a given range $[a, b)$.

```
int value_min = values[a];
for (int i=a+1; i<b; ++i)
{
    if ( values[i]<value_min )
        value_min = values[i];
}
```

The following code illustrates the computation of the sum of values in the same range [***a***, ***b***).

```
int sum = 0;
for (int i=a; i<b; ++i)
{
    sum = sum + values[i];
}
```

Each of these algorithms can be easily parameterized on the type of a data element. However, these variants of algorithms are not suitable for the parameterization of the representation of a semigroup with the type of a binary operation. Note that not only code inside bodies of these two loops is different, but also initializations and start positions of iterative processing.

The uniformity of the code of these algorithms can be achieved with the implementation based on functions that represent binary operations. If we introduce the functions for the minimum and addition of two values:

```
int BinaryOperationMin(int a, int b)
{
    int res = (b<a) ? b : a;
    return res;
}

int BinaryOperationAdd(int a, int b)
{
    int res = a + b;
    return res;
}
```

Then the algorithms that provide the same results as the operator-based variants can be written as follows:

```
int res = values[a];
for (int i=a+1; i<b; ++i)
{
    res = BinaryOperationMin(res, values[i]);
}
```

```
int res = values[a];
for (int i=a+1; i<b; ++i)
{
    res = BinaryOperationAdd(res, values[i]);
}
```

As we can see, now the only difference between two variants is the name of the function that represents a binary operation. In a more general form suitable for parameterized algorithms

```
int res = values[a];
for (int i=a+1; i<b; ++i)
{
    res = BinaryOperation(res, values[i]);
}
```

`BinaryOperation()` is any binary operation not only the minimum or addition of two values.

The variants of algorithms on basic data structures using functions of binary operations offer a higher level of the generality than operator-based variants. Despite this fact, they are a bit unusual in practice because they are normally less efficient than operator-based implementations.

5.12.2 Advanced Data Structures

The internal complexity of advanced data structures is a significant factor in the development of the efficient representation of a semigroup. Nevertheless, it should not divert our attention from the main task, which is the same as for basic data structures: achieve the uniformity of the concrete code to be parameterized.

The parameterization by the type of a data element is a straightforward task. The first version of an advanced data structure is written with concrete types. To convert an ordinary implementation into a template, we replace each concrete type with a template parameter. This can be done in one pass, but usually in several: one pass for each concrete type that we want to generalize.

As discussed earlier in this section, the parameterization by the type of a binary operation is less trivial even for basic data structures. The cost of not achieving this for basic data structures is tolerable in many practical situations. However, for advanced data structure the complications and consequences are much more serious because of the size and complexity of the implementation code. The parameterization of the representation of a semigroup with only one type of a binary operation is an important factor for achieving both the generality and efficiency.

The examples in this section illustrate algorithms on arrays or vectors using the subscript operator. The general purpose libraries offer iterator-based generic algorithms that can be applied to a wide variety of data structures. In the context of the design of efficient algorithms, the use of iterators is a programming implementation detail. Internal algorithms on data structures may not use iterators at all.

It is more important that all of the particular algorithms generated with a template for user-provided concrete types have the same computational path. And in each particular case the path is valid and, ideally, optimal for the specified operations. When we use a template to generate a particular algorithm, we obtain a path through a data structure that does not depend on concrete types. Thus, it might seem that the uniformity of the path is provided by a template. However, this is not completely correct. The level of the template generalization depends on the uniformity of the computational path that we achieve for concrete types at the design stage. The length of this uniform path determines the performance of the whole family of algorithms.

In basic data structures, the computational path is trivial. It is topologically equivalent to a chain of nodes in a linked list. All of the specific algorithms that compute the sum or find the minimum value in a given range visit the same nodes that store user data.

The advanced data structures, such as augmented level linked B+-trees, offer versatile facilities that take advantage of the complexity of the structure and the ability to store both user and implementation specific data. The shortest computational path is the key to providing the best performance. However, because of the complex connectivity different algorithms may use different paths. In this case, we will lose the generalization power of templates. In our efficient representation of a semigroup, the uniformity of the computational path is guaranteed by the finger search algorithm. All of the variants of fast algorithms that support different range queries use the same path through nodes of an augmented B+-tree. As discussed earlier, for range queries the sequence of nodes detected by finger search has the same importance as a linear chain of nodes in a linked list.

5.12.3 Computing Several Characteristics

To illustrate the difference between basic and advanced data structures, let us consider the computation of several characteristics of a data distribution in a given range. When a user dataset is stored in a basic data structure, such as an array, this can be accomplished in a single pass by applying to user data several appropriate binary operations:

```
sum = values[a];
min = values[a];
max = values[a];

for (int i=a+1; i<b; ++i)
{
    value = values[i];
    sum = BinaryOperationAdd(sum, value);
    min = BinaryOperationMin(min, value);
    max = BinaryOperationMax(max, value);
}
```

This method is space efficient but not time efficient, since it takes linear time.

The fast computation of the same characteristics of the same dataset involves a level linked B+-tree prepared with the method of multiple augmenting (see Figure 5.4). Given a class template that represents a semigroup, we introduce a user defined type for application specific data, which are pre-computed and stored in an internal node:

```
struct NodeData
{
    int sum;
    int min;
    int max;
    // ...
};
```

and a binary operation on these node data:

```
NodeData  BinOperationNodeData(
                NodeData a,
                NodeData b)
{
    NodeData res;
    res.sum = (a.sum+b.sum);
    res.min = (b.min<a.min) ? b.min : a.min;
    res.max = (b.max>a.max) ? b.max : a.max;
    return res;
}
```

After a user algorithm builds an object of a semigroup

```
SemiGroup semigroup(BinOperationNodeData);
// ...
```

it can obtain the sum, the minimum and the maximum in any range by calling the member function:

```
NodeData data_range;
data_range = semigroup.reduce(
                position_start,
                position_end);
```

The function `reduce()` implements the finger search algorithm, which applies `BinOperationNodeData()` to pre-computed data stored in nodes on the path. All of the result values are obtained in one pass because of multiple augmenting internal nodes with data, which are synchronized in space. In this particular algorithm, finger search can be regarded as an efficient method of sequential processing equivalent to the operator `for(;;)` in the algorithm using an array. Note also that there are several alternative names for this sort of functions. The most common are accumulate, aggregate, fold and reduce.

The important practical advantage of using templates for the implementation of advanced data structures is that adding a new particular data structure that supports a wide variety of fast algorithms involves the small additional cost of writing several lines of code, such as that for the function `BinOperationNodeData()`. In the real code, the implementation a function object is not much larger. This is significantly cheaper compared to developing a large amount of code for a new concrete advanced data structure. The generic programming technique offers not only the ease of implementation but also the ease of using templates in client code.

5.13 PERFORMANCE MEASUREMENTS

For practical applications of the efficient representation of a semigroup it is not sufficient to know only computational complexities of algorithms. It is also necessary to measure their real performance on specific computer systems in the context of suitability for user needs. The choice of the optimal representation and algorithms is a non-trivial task for several reasons.

The performance of programming implementations of algorithms on real systems is not always consistent with asymptotical computational complexities provided by abstract models. The algorithms do not directly access physical memory, which has a few levels of cache. Their running times are affected by the complex algorithms of virtual memory management. As a result, the cost of an operation, which is constant in a theoretical model, in practice is often a function of the problem size. The additional complication is that array-based and linked data structures have quite different performance characteristics.

The main question of practical interest is whether the efficient representation of a semigroup provides performance gain that follows from computational complexities of algorithms for range queries. Note that, unlike basic data structures, advanced data structures support two variants of computations using sequential processing of all of the elements in a given range and using the shortest path detected by finger search. This fact enables us to directly measure the required performance gain. It is expected that the running time of computations will be improved from linear to logarithmic.

The algorithms supported by the efficient representation of a semigroup were tested on a wide variety of computer systems: mobile devices, laptops, desktops and workstations. The operating systems tested were Windows and Android. Despite significant difference in the system parameters and in measured absolute values of running times, the performance gains have close values. The measured gain as a function of the input size complies with the expected gain $N/\log N$. This is a considerable performance improvement by orders of magnitude. A good consistency with the model estimates can be observed in a wide range of the input size, for example, from 500 to 500,000 data elements. When the input size exceeds a system specific limit, the performance gain deviates from theoretical prediction. This effect is normally caused by the increasing frequency of cache misses.

In terms of comparison against other data structures, an array is of special importance, since it is the fastest basic data structure for sequential processing of data. Because of highly efficient access to elements, an array is the main choice for small scale applications to compute characteristics of a dataset in a given range. However, an array is a potential trap that can cause performance degradation of a user algorithm when the scale of an application increases. When it comes to range queries, linear performance of sequential processing cannot compete against logarithmic provided by advanced data structures. The same linear performance of insert and delete operations on arrays is another important reason to consider alternative data structures.

5.14 DIFFICULTIES OF GENERALIZATION

The approach to achieving the generalization in the efficient representation of a semigroup that we have so far considered in principle is not too challenging. Nevertheless, it can be easily overlooked in the process of everyday software development. There are two reasons why binary operations may look unrelated. And these reasons are also the obstacles that preclude finding simple and useful generalizations in practice.

The first one is the difference in the specific terminology: In the context of the minimum value, we normally say "find the minimum value" or "search for the minimum value". In the context of the sum of values in a given range, we normally say "the computation or calculation of the sum of values". In the unified semigroup representation, we only say "the computation". It sounds a bit unusual for the minimum value, but this choice is more appropriate than "search for the sum of values".

The second obstacle is associated with the optimization of specific implementations for the best performance of algorithms on basic data structures. In this context, there is an important difference between comparison and arithmetic operators. A comparison operator returns a Boolean value: ***true*** or ***false***, whereas the result of the + operator is a value of the same type as operands. For large size values of operands, a comparison operator is generally faster than the + operator, since the size of a Boolean value is relatively small and fixed.

At the same time, the difference in the type of a result between comparison and arithmetic operators is responsible for the loss of uniformity of the operator-based implementations of algorithms that find the minimum or compute the sum of values.

The design of advanced data structures for the general purpose representations of mathematical concepts ignores small constant cost performance benefits. Instead, it concentrates on the significant reduction of the total number of operations. In order to avoid the trap of specific performance optimization, such as that of operator-based algorithms on basic data structures, we apply the top-down design method from a mathematical solution using the most abstract concepts to implementation in a programming language.

The alternative method of the bottom-up design and generalization based on programming concepts is much more risky. Programming is a relatively young field of science. The programming concepts are not so well formed compared to mathematical ones. The software libraries and tools developed by small groups of programmers are inevitably influenced by application specific concepts. It is not unusual that the process of the development ends up with the re-discovery of a fundamental concept, such as a set, which also offers a number of operations or algorithms to serve user needs. Such somewhat distorted generalizations are problematic not only for a novice but also for experienced developers who are new to a project.

Finding generalizations powerful and useful in practical applications is the hard work that can take significant amount of time of research and experimenting. In mathematics, this hard work has been already done for us by the best experts. This is why, mathematical concepts are the safe choice for solutions to numerous problems. The wide variety of basic and advanced data structures is required for the optimal performance of these solutions.

5.15 PREMATURE OPTIMIZATION

Achieving the right balance between generality and efficiency of programming solutions is related to the well-known issue of "premature optimization" considered in almost every book on algorithms and data structures. This issue is quite significant for the design and development of general purpose libraries. In the development of specific applications for end users, the problem should not arise at all. A well-managed project provides requirements for the performance characteristics of a product or a feature. Testing shows if the product meets the requirements or not. If at some stage of development the requirements are found to be a bit vague, it makes sense to discuss subtleties to avoid unnecessary optimization.

The correctness of a software product has the highest priority. The general purpose data structures and algorithms are reliable and versatile tools that provide performance sufficient for many types of real-world applications. The first version of a product or a prototype is normally based on such general purpose tools. When their performance becomes unacceptable, we start fine tuning algorithms. For an inefficiency caused by a basic data structure, there is a possibility to improve performance from linear to logarithmic by replacing it with an advanced data structures. In more challenging cases, we apply design methods of multiple augmenting and/or develop specialized solutions that take advantage of good knowledge of the application domain.

5.16 SUMMARY

In this chapter, we have discussed the efficient general purpose representation of a mathematical semigroup based on augmented level linked B+-trees. The new variant of these trees works with any number of associative binary operations and can compute main statistical characteristics of a data distribution in any given range of consecutive values: the sum, the mean, the standard deviation, the minimum and the maximum.

The representation of a semigroup discussed in this chapter has been designed and implemented by extending the efficient representation of a mathematical sequence. The new level of abstraction has been achieved without loss of efficiency. The representation of a semigroup provides all of the efficient operations on sequences developed previously. It makes no simplifying assumptions about order or duplicates in a given dataset.

The design method that enables us to add new efficient operations to a data structure is multiple augmenting. It eliminates the need to use several data structures with different performance characteristics, since all of the efficient operations required in a user algorithm can be provided by one data structure.

At a high level of abstraction, the separate description of the efficient representation of a semigroup and the fast summation algorithms is unnecessary, since a semigroup includes a summation as a special case. Nevertheless, the fast summation algorithms are fundamental to many practical applications and not all of them are appropriate for a semigroup. The discussion of different algorithms and subtleties associated with binary operations helps better understand various aspects of designing new efficient algorithms on advanced data structures.

The development and maintenance of a computer representation of a mathematical concept using an advanced data structure is generally a challenging task. Unlike basic data structures, both the size and the complexity of the code for advanced data structures are serious complicating factors. Generic programming is the technique that relieves us of the burden of this complexity. It supports high level generalizations in programming solutions with the optimal cost of development. In order to take advantage of templates, we reduce algorithms for different concrete types to a uniform implementation. At this design stage, we usually neglect small constant cost performance improvements in favour of simpler and more general algorithms. The high performance of new algorithms for range queries is guaranteed by the shortest computational path detected by finger search. All of the programming implementations of particular algorithms generated by a compiler for different types of binary operations use the same path through the nodes of an augmented level linked B+-tree.

For long term projects, the generic programming technique offers important practical benefits: the ease of implementation and the ease of using templates in client code. If a programming language does not provide facilities of generic programming the implementation of the general purpose representations of mathematical concepts is not impossible, but the development is quite costly and the generalization capacity is limited.

Compared to standard sequential processing, the new algorithms on augmented level linked B+-trees provide substantial performance improvement measured on a wide variety of computers, including modest systems and mobile devices.

The efficient representation of a mathematical semigroup demonstrates the significant potential of advanced data structures and modern programming techniques for solving important practical problems.

Chapter 6: Algorithms on Array-Based Data Structures

The explanation of the standard sequential summation algorithm is one the simplest tasks if we use a modern programming language that supports arrays. The situation is different, however, when we consider the fast sequential summation algorithms. The array-based variants of these algorithms are quite challenging. And this is the main reason why we started the description with augmented linked data structures.

The discussion of array-based variants of fast summation and related algorithms is interesting and worthwhile for several reasons: The basic principles of the design of algorithms are independent of their specific technical details, which vary widely from one implementation to another. This fact allows us to illustrate and analyze matching algorithms on an array representation of a data structure using a linked representation and vice versa. In order to appreciate this opportunity, compare the size of code. An implementation of an augmented level linked B+-tree may have several thousands of lines, whereas an algorithm on an array can be expressed in about ten lines. Another important practical advantage is that the array-based variants of data structures and algorithms provide the best performance in proper applications, which do not require a wide variety of operations on user data. The best-known example is the array representation of a complete binary tree and a binary heap.

One of the interesting results of our discussion is that we will arrive at the same summation algorithm, which was first proposed by Fenwick for the array representation of the data structure that was originally called Binary Indexed Tree. The attractive features of this algorithm are the small size of code and the ease of writing the implementation. However, these benefits come at the expense of the superficial simplicity. The data structure looks mysterious at first. Its implementation hides the ideas behind the fast algorithms. The implicit array representations of data structures are generally harder to understand than matching linked data structures. In addition, the algorithms on this data structure are difficult because it was originally designed for data compression. For a novice, it is not obvious how it works and what the limitations of the array representation are.

One of the main data structures and several algorithms that we discuss in this chapter were originally implemented using arrays. The graphical visualization has proven to be a powerful tool in the design of efficient array-based algorithms. However, except for basic data structures and sequential processing algorithms, preparing for the analysis meaningful illustrations with arrays is not a trivial task. As the complexity increases, the relationships between an advanced data structure and its underlying data structure become less transparent. In the representation of advanced data structures, arrays are often used as a space and time efficient storage that does not support explicit links. Any element of an array can be accessed in constant time, which implies that at the deepest implementation level each pair of elements in an array is connected by an implicit link. Because of this excessive connectivity, the key structural aspects may not be clearly seen in diagrams. The flat array storage hides the structural complexity and the depth of a data structure the array represents.

This difficulty of the visualization associated with the implicit nature of array representations is one of the reasons why the array-based variants are not the best choice for an introduction to efficient summation and other related algorithms. Instead, it would be more practical to use for this purpose a matching linked data structure that avoids issues of the implicit nature of array representations and helps us better understand fast array-based algorithms. In terms of the graphical representation, the important feature of a linked structure is that it supports one step at a time operations to access neighbours directly connected to a given node. This feature simplifies the illustration of the structure and the dynamics of algorithms. The alternative representations allow us to analyze efficient algorithms from different perspectives and provide insight into how these algorithms work.

The task of devising a matching data structure has the technical difficulty that an array representation and a linked representation of a data structure are never identical. Because of the significant difference in the space and time efficiency of the facilities, a single matching linked representation may not be fully adequate to explain fast algorithms on an array. It only enables us to understand a subset of operations on an array-based data structure. For this reason, the interpretation of one array representation of a data structure may involve more than one linked representation. In this aspect, such linked representations are auxiliary tools for the analysis and development of new efficient algorithms on arrays. These tools usually also include directed acyclic graphs that illustrate the dynamics of the algorithms or operations.

6.1 SEGMENT TREE

We start with the simple variant of a segment tree, which has the structure of a perfect binary tree. It is widely used in practical applications for efficient range queries. The key feature of this tree is the perfect balance. All of the levels of the tree are completely filled. Each parent node has exactly two children, thus, the total number of internal nodes in such a tree is $2^h - 1$, where h is its height. Because of these simple properties and ease of programming implementation, this segment tree is a popular choice for array representations and efficient array-based algorithms. The array implementation takes advantage of the rigid structure, in which a parent has the fixed number of children, and a simple computational method, which provides efficient access to any required position in the array.

The linked representation of the segment tree is also quite simple. Although it is less efficient than the array representation, it is more appropriate for the explanation of algorithms. We will use a level linked variant of this tree with the optimized support for sequences (see Figure 6.1), since one of the goals of this chapter is the introduction to fast summation algorithms. As we have already seen for augmented B+-trees, the fast summation algorithms can be easily obtained by the extension of the efficient representation of a sequence. For this reason, our initial discussion concentrates on the efficient counting and rank algorithms provided by the segment trees and related data structures that we will consider in this chapter.

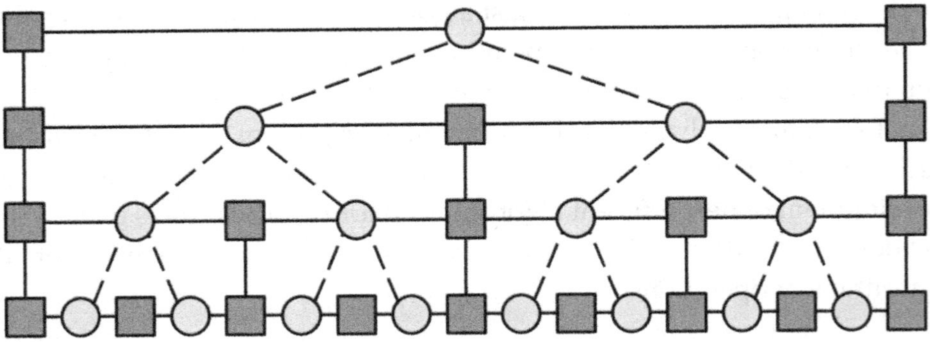

Figure 6.1: A level linked segment tree with the structure of a perfect binary tree. The child-parent relationships and links of the perfect binary tree are drawn with dotted lines.

The main data structure, which is shown in Figure 6.1, consists of square nodes connected by solid links. The rigid structure of this special tree is similar to that of level linked B+-trees discussed before. The data structure with dotted links is a standard perfect binary tree. It has been added to illustrate child-parent relationships between horizontal links of the main level linked data structure. These relationships suggest the names for the main data structure: a level linked segment tree or a level linked perfect binary tree.

One of the advantages of this level linked data structure over a standard perfect binary tree is that it is more suitable for the geometric interpretation and visualization of fast rank and summation algorithms. In the level linked representation of a segment tree, a horizontal link represents a line segment with the constraint that the length of a parent segment is equal to the total length of its child segments. The length of a segment at the deepest level is equal to 1. At each level up, it increases by a factor of 2 and equals a power of two 2^k. This feature of the level linked structure makes it ideal for algorithms using the binary representation of integer numbers. The length of a parent segment is proportional to the count of sequence elements in a sub-tree or the number of consecutive elements in a range of a given sequence.

Similar to a level linked B+-tree, this data structure is able to support shortest path algorithms. However, because of very small branching factor it is much higher than a typical B+-tree. The traversal of the relatively large number of vertical links makes noticeable contribution to the total running time of algorithms on such a data structure. Since a B+-tree supersedes a binary tree, the effect of this contribution on the performance of a level linked perfect binary tree can be easily estimated by reducing branching factor to the minimal possible in the implementation of a level linked B+-tree. Normally, there is no need to implement the level linked representation of a perfect binary tree. We discuss this representation only in the context of introduction to algorithms on arrays.

Despite the attractive properties associated with the relatively simple structure, a classical perfect binary tree it is not a practical data structure for the support of general purpose algorithms on datasets of arbitrary size. It is not the best choice for applications that frequently add or remove data elements. This type of a tree suffers from the fundamental limitation that its size 2^k-1 is fixed. In order to store an arbitrary number of data elements, a user algorithm needs to build a forest of binary trees of different sizes (see Figure 6.2). The main complicating factor is that the trees in such a forest are disconnected. The support for efficient search and traversal algorithms requires an ancillary data structure that represents a set of perfect binary trees. In terms of the implementation of a sequence, this approach is quite complex compared to a linked list or an array. This issue demonstrates the general disadvantage of perfect data structures: they do not provide sufficient flexibility in responding to client needs.

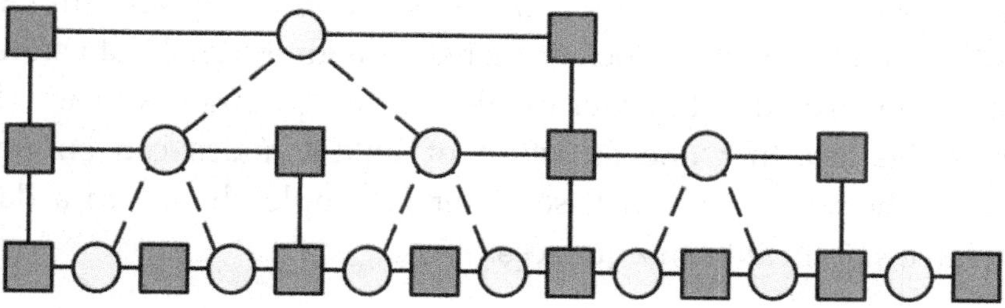

Figure 6.2: A forest of perfect binary trees (drawn with dotted links) and its representation using a level linked data structure (drawn with solid links).

The level linked data structure of square nodes (see Figure 6.2) is an alternative to the forest of perfect trees that are shown with dotted links.

The strength of this data structure is that its constituent level linked perfect binary trees are arranged into a simple linked list. It offers several advantages: The linked representation of the forest preserves the connectivity of all of the nodes at the deepest level that store elements of a given sequence. The connectivity of internal levels supports efficient shortest path algorithms between any two nodes of the data structure. The implementation of the linked representation does not have to maintain an ancillary data structure for a set of trees. It works for a sequence of an arbitrary size. The representation of the forest is also convenient for the visualization of algorithms. In this context, it represents a linear structure of connected segment trees.

As can be seen in Figure 6.2, the level linked data structure, which represents the forest of perfect binary trees, is not a level linked tree, it is a graph. Unlike a B+-tree, it is not globally balanced. This fact can make its implementation a bit more complex than that for a tree. Nevertheless, this data structure is quite simple to deal with the implementation problems of the forest. To simplify the discussion, we normally avoid the relatively complex representation of a forest and illustrate algorithms on level linked perfect binary trees.

6.2 DATA SCHEMES

One of the key questions that arises in the design of data structures and algorithms is how to make a data scheme effective. More specifically, the question is how to effectively associate user data with internal data stored in nodes of a data structure. In order to answer this question, we can take advantage of the fact that one structure of linked nodes can support different data schemes. As we will see later, a simple change to a data scheme can have significant consequences.

In this section, we will consider the following question: how to save in a level linked segment tree data required in a user algorithm. A node-based data structure provides two options for saving the length of a segment: either in the left or in the right node of a horizontal link. Thus, we have the choice between two possible data schemes.

Figure 6.3 shows a level linked segment tree with the main data scheme of this book. It has been previously used for the efficient representation of a mathematical sequence, which supports fast sequential summation algorithms. An important feature of this data scheme is that the accumulated data in internal nodes are designed to help a user algorithm to make the decision whether to move forward or not. In a level linked B+-tree, each internal node has a matching position in a linked list of the deepest level. The left and right nodes of a high level horizontal link define a range with a large number of consecutive elements at the deepest level. The efficient representation of a sequence that we considered before stores the count of elements in the left node of such a link. This count provides the distance between corresponding positions at the deepest level of a B+-tree. Forward traversing a high level link skips all of the elements of the deepest level in the range defined by the link. In this way, the main data scheme is optimized for forward sequential processing. The counts for reverse sequential processing are not stored in this data scheme. They can be obtained by moving to a previous node at the same level.

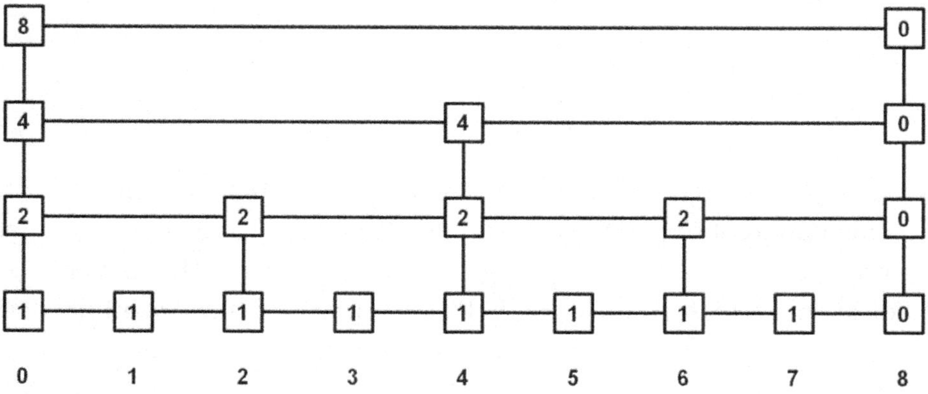

Figure 6.3: A level linked segment tree with the main data scheme based on a half-open range $[a, b)$. The count of sequence elements in a range is stored in the left node of a horizontal link.

Since the main data scheme at each level is based on a half-open range, in the discussion below we will pay special attention to properties of ranges in the context of the development of fast summation algorithms. Some aspects of this topic are simple and obvious, but they are a common source of confusion and errors in the code due to differences in interpretations and implementation approaches.

The algorithms of sequential processing are applied to all of the consecutive elements specified by the positions of the first and last elements. For an array, the positions are specified by integer indices. For sequences based on complex data structures, the positions are usually represented by iterators. The pair of end positions defines a range of positions and corresponding consecutive elements of a given sequence. A range is closed, if it includes its end positions. A range is open, if it does not include its end positions. A half-open range includes one end position.

The choice of a type of a range can have an important effect on the implementation of an algorithm. The half-open range [*a*, *b*) is one of the most widely used in programming solutions. It naturally supports forward sequential processing, such as shown in the code fragment below

```
// for an algorithm on an array
for (int i=a; i<b; ++i)
...

// alternative variant
for (int i=a; i!=b; ++i)
...
```

The key advantage of a half-open range is that it simplifies the implementation of sequential algorithms. With this choice, there is no need to write special code for processing of an empty range. This advantage is one of the main reasons for using half-open ranges in the algorithms of the standard library in C++. In order to offer a client the benefits of the wide variety of the standard algorithms, the data scheme shown in Figure 6.3 is compliant with the type of a half-open range specified by the standard library.

At the same time, it is necessary to note that the design decision to implement algorithms on half-open ranges is not absolutely safe. The support for a half-open range requires that the storage of a data structure provides one special dummy position after the last element of a user sequence. The value, which is stored at this position, is implementation specific and is invalid in the context of a user algorithm. Reading from or writing to this special storage position is not allowed. This implies that the choice of a half-open range comes at the cost of the potential problem of access violation. Note also that the sentinel technique, which uses a special value to terminate search algorithms, is not effective for the general purpose algorithms on unordered sequences.

The type of a half-open range, which we discussed above, includes left endpoint and excludes right endpoint: $[a, b)$. It has the extended name "left-closed, right-open". The second type of a half-open range excludes left endpoint and includes right endpoint: $(a, b]$. Its extended name is "left-open, right-closed". For brevity, we will name this type of a range "a reverse half-open range" because it is preferable for reverse sequential processing.

```
// for an algorithm on an array
for (int i=b; i>a; --i)
...

// alternative variant
for (int i=b; i!=a; --i)
...
```

Since the design of a data structure allows us to evaluate different data schemes to find the best one, it is interesting to consider the data scheme, which is based on a reverse half-open range. Its key feature is that the accumulated values are stored in the right node of a horizontal link (see Figure 6.4). Thus, in the efficient representation of a sequence the count of elements in an internal node provides the number of elements in a reverse range of a given sequence before the position at the deepest level defined by the internal node. The sum of values in this internal node, which is used by summation algorithms, is a characteristic of the same reverse range.

Despite the fact that this data scheme is more suitable for reverse sequential processing, it works with any type of a linked list, including a forward singly linked list. This is less convenient, but possible if a user algorithm saves a pointer to the current node and moves forward to read an accumulated value from the next node. Then, it can make the decision

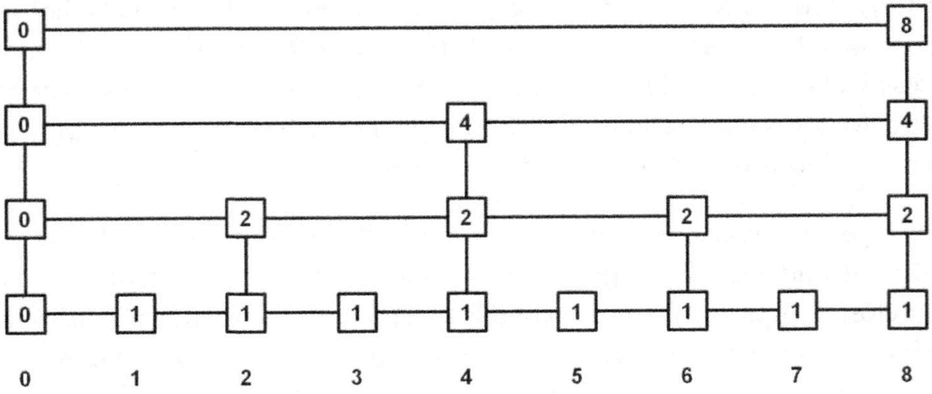

Figure 6.4: A level linked perfect binary tree with the data scheme based on a reverse half-open range (a, b]. The count of elements in a range is stored in the right node of a horizontal link.

whether to move forward or return to the saved node. For the general purpose algorithms, the reasonable connectivity is that of a doubly linked list. It can be effortlessly used with any data schemes discussed here, since it supports bidirectional traversal.

As discussed above, the support for a half-open range requires a special position in the storage, for which we either create a node in a linked list or allocate an additional cell in an array. The value at this position is implementation specific. In the case of a reverse half-open range, such a position in the storage is created before the first element of a given sequence. This operation moves all other nodes or cells, which store elements of the given sequence, to the right and, thus, increases the rank of each element of the given sequence by 1. For this reason, instead of zero-based indexing it is more convenient to use one-based indexing of elements of a given sequence.

The alternative of using standard zero-based indexing for given elements is possible too, but in this case the special position before the first element will have the negative rank -1. And this might not be the best option for the representation of a mathematical sequence, which is defined on the set of non-negative integers.

In the general case, reverse processing on a half-open range is not as trivial as it might seem at first glance. In order to relieve programmers of the burden of dealing with error prone code, well-designed libraries provide reverse iterators. Such an iterator is normally implemented using a matching forward iterator. One interesting detail is that the current position of a reverse iterator coincides with the previous position of its matching forward iterator.

The data scheme based on a reverse half-open range also supports fast sequential summation. The change of a data scheme does not change the length of a shortest path, which is a characteristic of the structure (connectivity of nodes). However, at this stage the data scheme based on a reverse half-open range does not look attractive for the development of fast summation algorithms. It does not offer advantages over the main data scheme based on a forward half-open range. The additional complication is that the straightforward combination of algorithms on forward and reverse half-open ranges in not safe because of different indexing. A forward half-open range $[a, b)$ is sufficient for most simple and typical tasks. It makes unnecessary duplication of algorithms on a reverse half-open range, which is more error prone in programming solutions. Unsurprisingly, a reverse half-open range is relatively rarely used in algorithms. Nevertheless, the data scheme based on a reverse half-open range offers interesting opportunities for developing fast array-based algorithms, which we will consider below.

6.3 MODIFIED SEGMENT TREE

The level linked segment tree with the structure of a perfect binary tree allows for the time and space efficient array representation. However, it is not the best choice to develop algorithms on datasets of arbitrary sizes. To avoid implementation complexity of a forest of perfect binary trees, we need another data structure that addresses this issue and supports a simple array representation. It appears that the goal can be achieved with a new data structure that can be derived from the level linked segment tree.

The required modification is based on two observations. The first one is simple: Each parent stores the accumulated value, which is the sum of values of its children. In a binary tree, the value of one child enables us to compute the value of another child. Thus, a fast counting or summation algorithm can work even if a modified tree stores values of one child only. The second observation is a bit less obvious: for the best performance, a fast counting or summation algorithm should avoid traversal of horizontal links of second children, because it makes a path longer compared to a path through proper parents. These facts imply that we can remove from a level linked segment tree each horizontal link of a second child. Note that saving space is not the main goal of this modification to the original data structure. It is a means of building the new data structure that allows for a relatively simple array representation. Figure 6.5 illustrates the data structure obtained from the level linked segment tree shown in Figure 6.4.

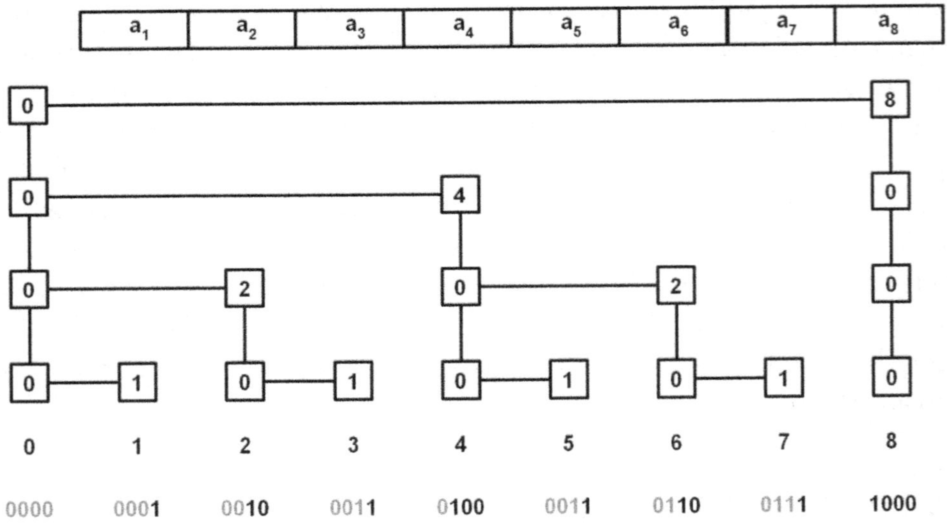

Figure 6.5: A data structure derived from a level linked segment tree (see Figure 6.4) by removing every second child link. The right node of a horizontal link stores the count of sequence elements in a range. The left node stores zero value. The bottom line shows the least significant 1 bits of indices of values, which match 1 bits in vertical chains.

6.4 PROPERTIES OF NEW LINKED DATA STRUCTURE

As we have seen earlier, the efficient representations of a sequence are based on augmented balanced trees, whereas the simplest representations of a sequence use linked lists. The new linked data structure is another interesting example of using a non-linear structure to achieve high performance for operations on data associated with a given sequence. Below we discuss the main properties of this data structure.

6.4.1 Connectivity

The data structure obtained after the removal of every second horizontal child link is a binary tree with the connectivity of nodes known as left-child, right-sibling. This connectivity has the following simple properties. All of the children of a parent are organized in a linked list at the same level of the tree. The first (leftmost) child is directly connected to its parent. All other children are not directly connected to the parent. This highly flexible connectivity gives a binary tree the ability to support complicated data structures, such as a tree with arbitrary numbers of children and a forest of trees as an ordered set of trees. This ability is particularly important for developing fast summation algorithms on arrays, since it enables us to overcome the limitation of a perfect binary tree on the size of a given sequence.

The price of this flexibility is that the new data structure is not a level linked tree, since each level is no longer a completely linked list. Two children of each parent are connected by a horizontal link, but there are no links between children of different parents. This data structure is not the best choice for the algorithms that require efficient sequential processing, because the deepest level is not a linked list. The strength of this binary tree is that its relatively small set of links is still good enough for fast top-down and bottom-up traversal of the data structure. In combination with its ability to support a forest as one connected component, the tree guarantees that a user algorithm can efficiently reach any node of the tree from any other node.

In order to visually check that a tree, such as shown in Figure 6.5, is binary, it is recommended to rotate a diagram by 45 degrees clockwise. Such a rotation, however, might be misleading for the analysis of efficient algorithms. The rotated tree would have the height linear in the number of sequence elements, which does not explain the high performance of the algorithms supported by the tree.

The new data structure is not perfectly balanced, when it represents a forest of constituent trees with different heights. The last tree may contain one data elements only, whereas the first tree contains all other elements. The difference in the heights of these trees has no effect on the worst case performance, since it is determined by the number of levels, which is logarithmic in the size of a given sequence. This feature guarantees the high performance of algorithms based on the shortest path, including search and summation.

As an example of the worst case scenario, consider the task of finding a path between two nodes of the deepest level that store two elements of a given sequence. When the elements are quite distant, the simple approach to achieve logarithmic performance is to select a path between the proper nodes through the top level of the structure. Normally, the path connecting two nodes of the deepest level is shorter because two bottom-up paths intersect at a common ancestor before reaching the top level of the tree.

6.4.2 Data Scheme

According to the data scheme based on a reverse half-open range, only the right node of a horizontal link stores data associated with a given sequence. For the fast rank algorithm, such a node stores a positive count of sequence elements. For the fast summation algorithms, a right node also stores the sum of values of sequence elements. The right nodes play the main role in providing required data to a user algorithm. The value of the count stored in such a node is a power of 2. It represents the least significant 1 bit in the binary representation of an integer number. For brevity, we refer to such a node as a 1 bit node.

The left node of a horizontal link corresponds to the left endpoint of a reverse half-open range in a given sequence. This node stores an implementation specific value not allowed to be used in client algorithms. Such values do not make any contribution to the result of the rank or summation algorithm. Thus, we construct all of the left nodes with the values of counts and sums set to zero. In terms of the binary representation of an integer number, such a node is a 0 bit node. Despite the fact that the left nodes do not store data associated with a given sequence or with structural invariants, they are important for maintaining the entire structure connected, traversing the structure and providing efficient access to accumulated data.

6.4.3 Sequence of Vertical Chains

For the analysis of algorithms, it is often helpful to view the new linked data structure as a sequence of vertical chains of nodes connected by horizontal links at different levels. A vertical chain of nodes is a constituent part of this data structure similar to that in the level linked B+-trees and the level linked segment trees considered before. The transformation that destroys the connectivity of linked lists of levels does not destroy the connectivity of vertical chains, although it has an effect on the counts stored in nodes of such chains.

In terms of the connectivity, a vertical chain has only one link from the top node to a previous node at the same level. Any other lower node is either not linked or linked to a next node at the same level, which is the top node of another vertical chain. Thus, one vertical chain can be connected to more than one next vertical chain by proper horizontal links.

As for the data stored in nodes of a vertical chain, only the top node is a 1 bit node. It is the right node of a horizontal link, which stores accumulated data: a positive count of sequence elements and the sum of their values. All other nodes in this chain are left nodes or 0 bit nodes, which store zero values of counts and sums. Thus, each vertical chain of nodes provides the binary representation of an integer count in the top node, which is a power of 2. The number of 0 bit nodes is equal to the number of trailing zeros in the count of the top node.

As it can be seen, such a vertical chain represents the least significant 1 bit of an integer number. But the important detail is that this 1 bit is the least significant 1 bit of an integer index into the sequence of the vertical chains.

The following rows show indices in the decimal and binary representations and values of least significant bits:

index:	0,	1,	2,	3,	4,	5,	6,	7,	8,
	0000,	0001,	0010,	0011,	0100,	0101,	0110,	0111,	1000,
LS 1 bit:	0000,	0001,	0010,	0001,	0100,	0001,	0010,	0001,	1000,
	0,	1,	2,	1,	4,	1,	2,	1,	8,

In terms of data, the sequence of vertical chains is also the sequence of the least significant 1 bits of indices.

Similar to its prototype (see Figure 6.4), the new linked data structure shown in Figure 6.5 is intrinsically two dimensional. The scale of the horizontal dimension is linear, whereas the scale of the vertical dimension is logarithmic. Because of this feature, the data structure supports two representations of an integer number, which is a power of 2. The length of a horizontal segment, which is represented by a link, is proportional to the size of a range in a given sequence. The height of a vertical chain is logarithmic in the range size. Thus, a vertical chain of nodes is a space efficient alternative to a long horizontal segment. The ability to provide two representations of an integer number is convenient for the analysis of different aspects of algorithms, since we can choose whichever is more suitable for the count in a 1 bit node, which is also the size of a range in a given sequence.

6.4.4 Partitioning Method

In terms of the connectivity of nodes, the new linked data structure represents a binary tree, which supports efficient access to data. The other important characteristic of this data structure is the method of arranging the data for fast counting and summation algorithms. This method will become clear when we analyze the relationships between the data stored in the structure. This analysis quickly reveals that the new linked data structure cannot be viewed as a classical binary tree, such as a segment tree, since every second horizontal child link is absent. Each parent segment covers only one child segment at the next level down. Such parent-child relationships are not typical for binary trees.

In order to better understand properties of this linked data structure, it is necessary to consider all of the segments at different levels directly underneath one segment at a high level. As we move down to the deepest level, the length of a segment quickly decreases. The sequence of lengths of these segments represents a geometric progression:

$$(2^{k-1}, 2^{k-2}, \ldots, 2^1, 2^0)\ ;$$

The sum of the geometric progression plus 1 is equal to 2^k, which is the length of the segment that covers this ordered sequence of non-overlapping segments. It means that if we add the missing last segment of unit length, the resulting sequence of segments would represent a complete partition of the parent segment. Since a segment represents a range, the incomplete sequence of segments provides the required implementation specific partition of a large range in a given sequence. The fact that the covered segments are ordered is important to mirror the binary representation of an integer number, which is a power of 2. The position of a covered segment in such an ordered sequence is determined by its level.

The partition of a segment into an ordered sequence of covered segments is the key method of data organization in the new linked data structure. For maintaining the structural invariants, the partitioning is applied to segments of all levels, except for the deepest one. In terms of parent-child relationships, the partition does not have a fixed number for child segments in the sequence. The number depends on the length of the parent segment. This feature, however, does not affect the performance of main operations because the size of the partition is logarithmic in the size of a given sequence in the worst case. In this aspect, the new linked data structure is different from balanced trees, which place the restriction on the maximum number of children. The logarithmic size of the partition guarantees high performance of algorithms using data accumulated for the partition ranges, such as counts and sums.

The partition of one range of size 2^k into an ordered sequence of adjoining non-overlapping ranges can be easily demonstrated with the diagram for the flat array representation of this linked data structure, which does not need vertical links. In such a diagram, both parent and children ranges would be at the same level of the array storage. This illustration, however, is ineffective for the whole array representation, which partitions each range of size greater than 1. To avoid confusion, Figure 6.6 illustrates the partition of an array into subarrays, which uses the method of partitioning horizontal segments shown in Figure 6.5. This diagram takes advantage of the fact that a linked data structure arranges segments at different levels and, thus, helps us better visualize the array partition.

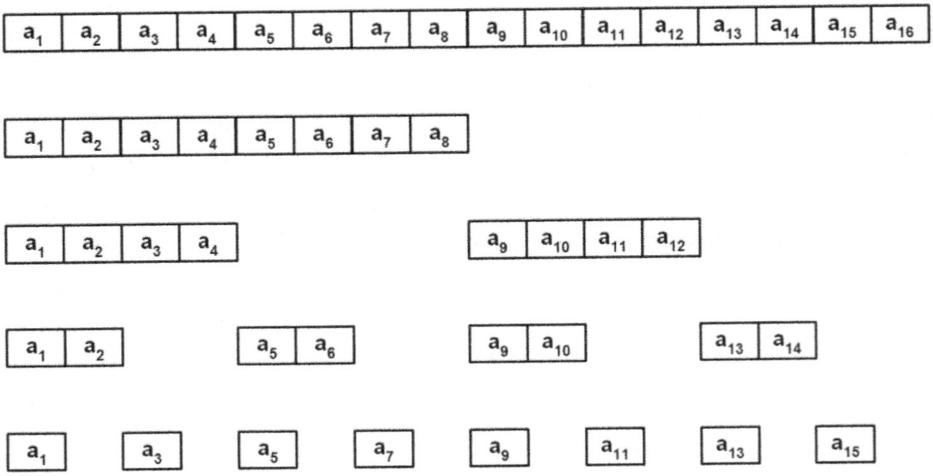

Figure 6.6: The partition of an array into subarrays using the method for linked data structures shown in Figure 6.5. Each subarray corresponds to a reverse semi-open range defined by a horizontal link in an appropriate linked data structure.

6.5 OPTIMIZED ARRAY OF SUMS

The visual examination shows that both prototype and resulting data structures have the same number of nodes (see Figure 6.4 and Figure 6.5). It is interesting that the removal of each second child link from a level linked segment tree does not change the total number of nodes. However, this transformation causes the important side-effect, which is not immediately obvious. In a level linked segment tree (see Figure 6.4), the number of nodes that store accumulated data is twice the size of a given sequence minus one. After the removal of each second child link (see Figure 6.5), the number of nodes with accumulated data becomes equal to the size of a given sequence. This fact suggests that all of the data that are stored in 1 bit nodes of the new linked data structure can be saved in an array of the same size as a given sequence. In our data scheme based on a reverse half-open range, one additional cell is required to support one-based indexing of elements of a given sequence

The method for building the array representation of the new linked data structure (see Figure 6.5) follows from the observation that in each vertical chain there is only one 1 bit node, which is the top of the chain. The data in this 1 bit node, which are associated with a given sequence, must be saved in an array representation. All other nodes in the chain store implementation data specific only to the linked representation of the new data structure. These data are not required in the array representation of the new data structure. In terms of horizontal links, this observation means that each right node has one matching position and cell in the array representation. In the resulting array, the cell to save data from a 1 bit node is determined by the rank of the vertical chain that contains the 1 bit node.

The vertical dimension of this new linked data structure is not preserved in the array representation. In this respect, the array implementation is flat. There is no need to store vertical links and counts of sequence values, since an array provides constant time access to any cell, which is combined with the efficient computation of the position required in a user algorithm. The additional benefit is that the array representation is more space efficient compared to the new linked data structure.

6.5.1 Data Organization

Given the partition of an array into subarrays, such as shown in Figure 6.6, the task of developing the array that supports fast summation algorithms requires completing one step only. It is necessary to sum up values in each subarray and save a result in a proper cell. Figure 6.7 illustrates the array of sums for a given sequence of values. At this stage, we focus mainly on the data organization, because there are different methods and algorithms to build such an array from a given sequence or input data.

The diagram shows how a user algorithm can find the proper position to save a computed sum. In the array at the bottom of the diagram, the sum is stored at the position matching the rightmost cell of a subarray. The computed sum is the sum of all values in a range before and including its right endpoint.

This is a consequence of our choice of the data scheme based on a reverse half-open range. Another consequence of this choice is that the resulting array supports one-based indexing with the additional zero value in the first cell.

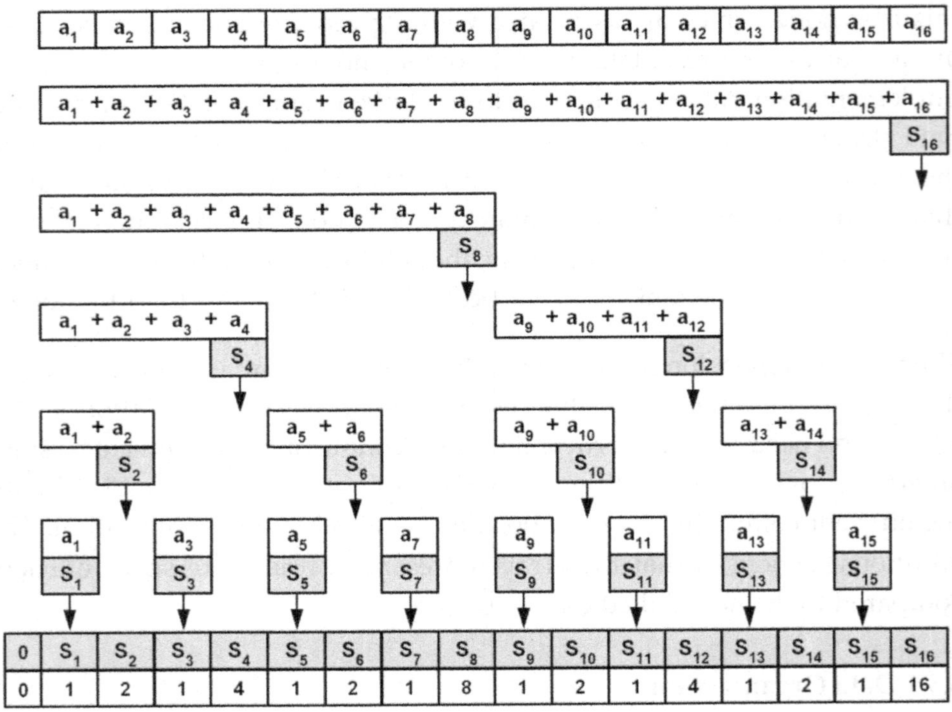

Figure 6.7: The organization of data in the array that support fast summation algorithms. The array at the top of the diagram is a given sequence. The partition of this array into subarrays is shown in Figure 6.6. Each subarray is reduced to a sum of its values. The position of the sum in the resulting array is determined by the position of the last (rightmost) value in the subarray. The resulting array of computed sums is shown at the bottom of the diagram in gray cells.

The interesting feature of this data organization is that the data, which are sequentially packed in the cells of the resulting array, are from different levels of the matching linked data structure. This array representation is quite different from that for a complete binary tree, which is constructed in the level by level order: the first cell stores data from the root, the second and third cells store root children data, then four cells with children data of the next level and so on.

It is also important to note that the resulting array of sums it is not an independent data structure, it is derived from a given sequence of values. Its use in practical solutions involves the risk of the data inconsistency. To avoid this problem, the accumulated data must be properly updated or re-computed when the given sequence is modified.

6.5.2 Comparison with Array of Partial Sums

The array-based data structure that we developed for fast summation algorithms may be a bit intriguing at first. This is both a disadvantage and a barrier to its effective use in practical applications. It does not appear to be as simple as the well-known array of partial sums. To ease understanding, we will compare these two types of array-based data structures. The goal of this section is to highlight the distinctive features of the new data structure.

The array-based data structure for fast summation algorithms can be viewed as an optimized variant of the table of partial sums. In the well-known basic variant of such a table, each array cell stores the sum of values from the first position in a given sequence to the current position:

array[i] = sum(values[1, i]);

Figure 6.8 illustrates the data organization in an array of pre-computed partial sums.

One of the practical issues of this table is linear running time of the update operation. The optimized variant of a table of range sums addresses this issue by guaranteeing logarithmic performance for both the update operation and the partial sum algorithm. The improvement comes from using a different set of ranges to compute and store the sum of values for a specified position in a sequence. Although the new summation algorithm is bit slower against the basic variant, the improvement of the overall performance of a user algorithm can be quite significant, since the optimized data structure solves the problem of a frequent inefficient operation.

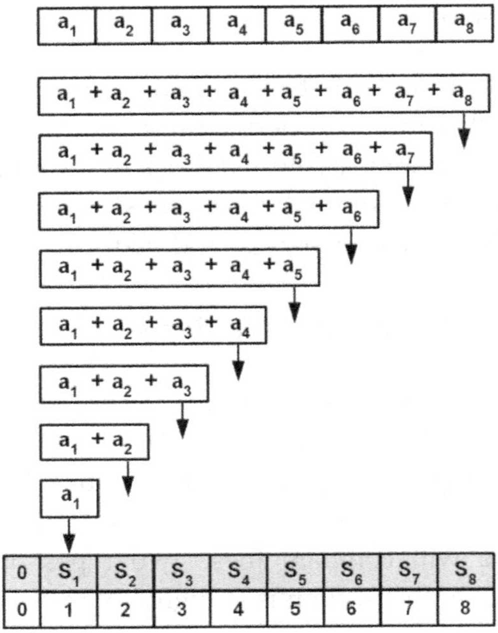

Figure 6.8: The diagram of the computation of an array of partial sums. The array at the top of the diagram is a given sequence. The resulting array of partial sums is shown at the bottom of the diagram in gray cells. The size of a range determines the position of a partial sum in the resulting array.

The linear performance of primary operations is a typical problem of basic data structures. We have already considered one of the main approaches to solving this problem with the augmented balanced trees, such as B+-trees. The array-based data structure that we discuss here offers yet another interesting and effective method of the data organization that enables us to deliver high performance of both required operations. This method is different from the methods used in the basic table of partial sums and in augmented balanced trees.

The inefficiency of the update operation on the basic table is caused by the fact that one value of a given sequence on average contributes to N/2 partial sums. A balanced tree avoids excessive re-computations and provides much better performance because its height is logarithmic in the size of a given sequence. To improve performance of the update operation without losing high efficiency of summation, the implementation of the new data structure needs a similar method of the data organization. It should provide the set of ranges that reduces from linear to logarithmic the number of contributions of each sequence value to the sums stored in the table.

This goal is achieved with the partition of a given sequence into the set of ranges associated with the binary representation of integer indices into the implementation array. For each index into the array, the corresponding range is defined by the least significant 1 bit in the binary representation of the index. In the equivalent form using the number of trailing zeros ***t***, the range is $[i - 2^t + 1, i]$ and has size 2^t. The simple definition, which is consistent with the data scheme based on a reverse half-open range, is that the range includes 2^t consecutive values before and at the current position in a sequence.

Similar to the basic table of partial sums, in the optimized table each partition range of a given sequence is represented by one value, which is the sum of all values in this partition range. Each partition range provides one accumulated value for the optimized table. Same as in the basic table, the position in the array of range sums to store the accumulated value is defined by the right endpoint of a partition range:

$$\text{array}[i] = \text{sum}(\ \text{values}[i - 2^t + 1, i]\ );$$

As we can see, the difference from the array of partial sums is only in the choice of the left endpoint of a range (compare also Figure 6.7 and Figure 6.8). However, the consequences of this difference are quite important.

The new partition ranges are significantly smaller than the partial sum ranges of the basic table. The average range size in the optimized table of sums is logarithmic in the size of a given sequence, whereas in the basic table it is linear. Because of the significantly smaller sizes of partition ranges, the computation of the accumulated values is much faster than in the basic table of partial sums. Along with the fact that the right endpoint of a partition range [i - 2^t +1, i] is equal to the index [i] into the array of range sums, it means that the definition of a partition range can be used for the straightforward sequential construction of such an optimized array of sums. The running time of this construction algorithm is linearithmic (O(N log N)). It is less efficient than the bottom-up construction algorithm, which takes linear time. This algorithm is considered below.

6.5.3 Terminology for Tables of Sums

The different choice of a summation range also suggests for the tables of sums the following terminology, which indicates the type of a range. In the computation of a partial sum, a range [1, index] is defined by an index into an array. The left endpoint of the range or the lower summation limit is fixed. Because of the one-to-one correspondence between an index and a computed sum, the partial sum stored at the position referred to by the index can be called ***Index Range Sum*** and the table of partial sums can be called ***Index Range Sums***. In the optimized table of sums, a summation range is defined by the least significant 1 bit of an integer index. For this reason, the similar name for the range sum might be ***Index Bit Range Sum*** and for the table of sums - ***Index Bit Range Sums***.

Both ***Index*** and ***Bit*** in these names are associated with the number of consecutive values in a summation range. The index provides the number of first values in a sequence, which is required for the computation of a partial sum. The index can be any positive integer less than or equal to the size of a given sequence. The partition into summation ranges based on the least significant 1 bits of integer indices implies that the number of sequence values is a power of 2. The names, which hint at the numbers of sequence values in the computations of sums, are consistent with the idea of developing fast summation algorithms as an extension of fast counting algorithms by removing the restriction that each value be equal one.

6.5.4 Navigation Method

The partition of a sequence into the set of smaller ranges of sizes, which are powers of 2, implies that a partial sum of an arbitrary number of sequence values can be computed as a sum of pre-computed sums. The algorithm is expected to be highly efficient, because the number of the pre-computed sums is equal to the number of the partition ranges that cover the range for a required partial sum. In order to implement this idea, we need a navigation method to efficiently access the pre-computed sums for proper partition ranges of the given sequence. One of the main advantages of the optimized variant of the table described above is that it supports very efficient traversal and access to data stored in the implementation array. For our algorithms, we need two traversal operations that involve the removal and the addition of the least significant 1 bit. They are normally implemented using simple and highly efficient bitwise operations on integer indices. The specific details vary from one system to another. They are important for the performance optimization, but less significant for understanding of the algorithms discussed here.

Since the least significant 1 bit of an integer index defines the size of a range, the bitwise operations have the simple interpretation. The distance to a next position is equal to the range size that corresponds to the least significant 1 bit. It means that the other simple option to move to the next position in the implementation array is to subtract or add the range size, which is a power of 2. This use of arithmetic operations on indices can help us make the implementation code more readable.

6.6 MATCHING LINKED DATA STRUCTURE

To continue comparative analysis of efficient algorithms, we need a linked data structure that matches the resulting array of sums shown in Figure 6.7. This goal can be easily achieved if we apply the method of augmenting to the data structure shown in Figure 6.5. Following this method, we compute for each partition range the new datum, which is the sum of sequence values. Thus, the new linked data structure stores not only the counts of sequence values but also the sums of these sequence values. The range sum augmenting is applied to 1 bit nodes only, 0 bit nodes store zero values of counts and sums. The linked data structure required for the discussion of algorithms is shown in Figure 6.9.

The reasons why each 1 bit node stores both the count and the sum of sequence values in a partition range are the same as for augmented B+ trees. A data structure without sums does not support fast summation algorithms. At the same time, a data structure with pre-computed range sums but without counts does not provide an efficient rank algorithm to access the sums associated with a given sequence. Only a combination of these two types of accumulated values in one data structure guarantees high performance of algorithms.

a_1	a_2	a_3	a_4	a_5	a_6	a_7	a_8
a[1]	a[1,2]	a[3]	a[1,4]	a[5]	a[5,6]	a[7]	a[1,8]
S_1	S_2	S_3	S_4	S_5	S_6	S_7	S_8

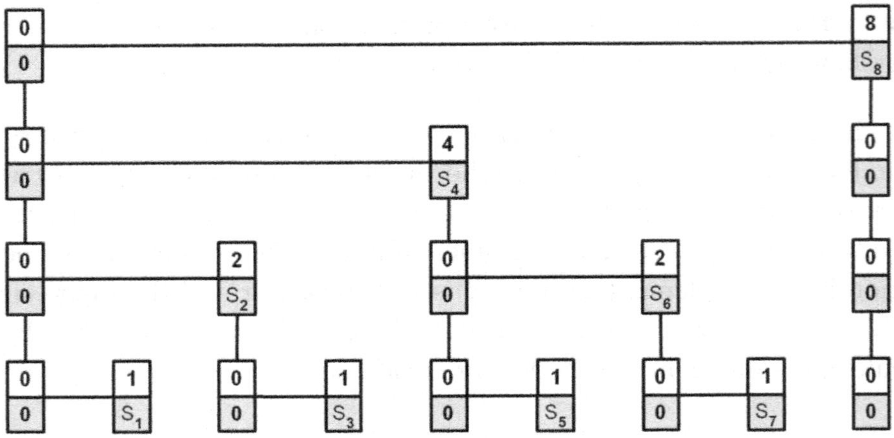

Figure 6.9: The linked representation of the array of sums shown in Figure 6.7. A 1 bit node stores a nonzero count and a sum of values in a partition range of a given sequence. A 0 bit node stores zero values of the count and the sum. This data structure represents an augmented variant of the data structure shown in Figure 6.5.

6.7 GENERALIZATION FOR ARRAY-BASED AND LINKED DATA STRUCTURES

The linked data structure shown in Figure 6.5 has been obtained from the well-known segment tree. Thus, it has some properties similar to the predecessor and can be viewed as a special type of a segment tree. At the same time, the differences between these two types of trees are significant and to distinguish from one another we need a name that reflects the main specifics of the new data structure. We prefer for this purpose the data organization to the connectivity. In this context, the key interesting feature of the new linked data structure is its partitioning method. A range of values is defined by the least significant 1 bit of an index into a sequence. This consideration suggests one of the possible names that matches the key features of the new linked data structure: ***index bit segment tree***. Using in this name the term ***bit*** seems to be more appropriate than ***binary***, since ***bit*** is associated with the ***binary*** representation of an integer number. The term ***bit*** is also more specific and accurate than ***binary***, which is quite widely used in the literature for various types of trees.

The data structure shown in Figure 6.5 stores only counts of values, which are internal structural invariants. In terms of user data, it represents an empty storage, which provides efficient access to accumulated data that will be saved in its nodes. Figure 6.9 shows an example of a data structure that stores sums of values of a given sequence. Such a data structure can be regarded as an ***augmented index bit segment tree***, which represents a table of partition range sums.

Given two new data structures (see Figure 6.7 and Figure 6.9), which are expected to be quite efficient to replace basic data structures in user algorithms, we can introduce the generalization for which these data structures provide the array and linked representations. The generalized definition is expected to express the main commonality between two representations. In this context, each new data structure can be viewed as the table of pre-computed sums, which is derived from a given sequence and represents an implementation sequence of sums of values of the given sequence in the partition ranges defined by the least significant 1 bits of integer indices into the implementation sequence using one-based indexing. Although the definition seems to be a bit long, it covers the key features of both array-based and linked data structures.

6.8 FAST COMPUTATION OF PARTIAL SUM

We begin our discussion of algorithms on the optimized table of sums with the fast computation of a partial sum. These summation algorithms help us better understand the properties of the new data structure, because they are relatively simple and similar to algorithms on augmented level linked B+-trees that we considered before.

Since counting of sequence values mirrors the summation of the corresponding indexed values

rank of 7th value: 1 + 1 + 1 + 1 + 1 + 1 + 1;

partial sum of 7 values: A1 +A2 +A3 +A4 +A5 +A6 +A7;

our first idea to design a fast partial sum algorithm was to extend the fast rank algorithm. The straightforward approach to implementing this idea is to replace count values of 1 with the indexed sequence values.

For an augmented level linked B+-tree, this approach does not deliver the desired result, since without counts the resulting tree is no longer an efficient sequence. To avoid this problem, it is necessary to add to each internal node the sum of values that correspond to the count of values stored in this node. The appropriate tree stores two matching datasets of accumulated values.

The simple idea of promoting a fast counting algorithm to a new level of generality, however, works for arrays, which are efficient sequences supported by a system. Their constant-time access to any element is much more efficient than that provided by counting algorithms, which guarantee logarithmic time only. This feature makes redundant storing in arrays counts of sequence elements and allows algorithms to operate on pre-computed sums directly through the subscript operator.

The optimized table of pre-computed sums supports a number of partial sum algorithms that mirror the binary representation of the rank of the last value in a specified summation range. The high performance is determined by the data organization: the sums in the table are associated with the least significant 1 bits of indices. A fast algorithm on such a table uses the binary representation of the index of the last value to find the matching binary representation of a partial sum:

rank of 7th value: 4+ 2+ 1;

partial sum of 7 values: (A1+A2+A3+A4)+(A5+A6)+A7;

In the description of sequences based on augmented linked data structures, we emphasized the importance of efficient counting and rank algorithms. For this reason, our primary interest is in algorithms using counting of sequence elements, which are equivalent to those on augmented linked trees.

The comparison of the array and linked representations is based on the intrinsic property of a linked index bit segment tree that each shortest path between any given node of the deepest level and the first node of the top level provides an ordered sequence of bits and thus the binary representation of the rank of the given node (see Figure 6.10).

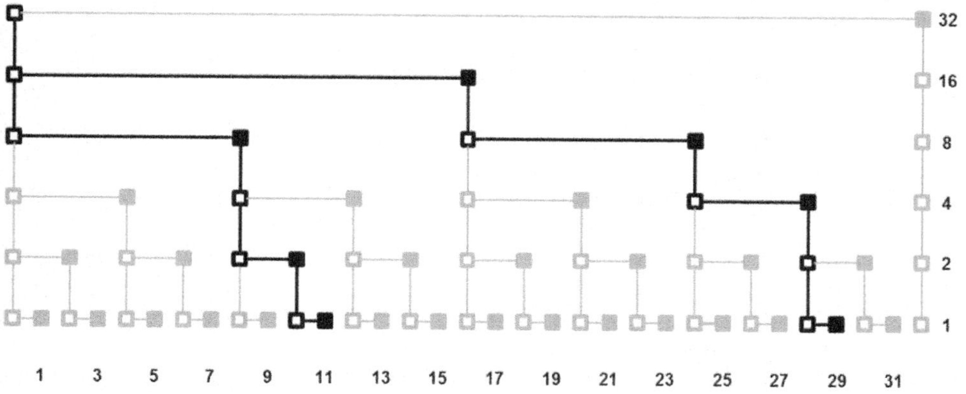

Figure 6.10: Illustration of shortest paths in a linked index bit segment tree. 0 bit nodes are empty, 1 bit nodes are filled.

Regardless of whether the traversal is top-down or bottom-up, each level contributes to a result of counting at most one nonzero value, which is a power of 2 and is stored in the right (1 bit) node of a horizontal link. Alternatively, a change in the total count is associated with the traversal of a horizontal link. For the ranks of nodes at the deepest level chosen in Figure 6.10, the paths provide the following sequences of bits:

11=(001011)=0x32+0x16+1x8+0x4+1x2+1x1= 8+2+1;

29=(011101)=0x32+1x16+1x8+1x4+0x2+1x1=16+8+4+1;

6.8.1 Top-Down Algorithm

The first array-based algorithm for the computation of a partial sum is equivalent to the top-down summation algorithm on augmented level linked segment trees and B+-trees. The computational path of this algorithm in the new linked data structure is illustrated in Figure 6.10.

```
int sum_top_down(const int k)
{
    int sum = 0;
    int count = 0;
    int bit = 1<<30;

    for (bit=1<<30; count<k; bit>>=1)
    {
        if ( k&bit )
        {
            count += bit;
            sum += m_array[count];
        }
    }

    return sum;
}
```

This algorithm scans the sequence of bits of the binary representation of the input rank `k` and reads accumulated values from the array of sums `m_array[]` to compute the sum of first `k` values. In more detail, the algorithm works as follows. The code uses the variable `bit`, which is a power of 2 and has a single 1 bit during the execution of the algorithm. This test bit is initialized to the most significant 1 bit of 32-bit integer (`1<<30`) and is shifted by the operation `bit>>=1` (division by 2). The operation `(k&bit)` is used to select the data associated with the bits in the binary representation of the rank `k`. All of the computations of a result are performed when the value of a current bit of `k` is 1.

The variable `count` accumulates the number of first sequence elements that have been already processed. It also represents a current position in the implementation array. Each iteration increases its value by the size of a current partition range of a given sequence `count+=bit`. Simultaneously, a pre-computed sum of values in the same range is added to the result of this algorithm `sum += m_array[count]`.

This algorithm is the simplest to demonstrate that the fast summation of sequence values parallels the fast summation of values of 1in the computation of a count or a rank. For clarity, the computation of the resulting sum in the next two lines of code:

```
count += bit;
sum += m_array[count];
```

can be re-written using the array position `pos` and range parameters of the size `range_size` and pre-computed sum `range_sum`:

```
pos = count;
range_size = bit;
// summation of values of 1
pos += range_size;
range_sum = m_array[pos];
// summation of sequence values
sum += range_sum;
```

The linked index bit segment tree provides the equivalent summation algorithm, which is based on the search for a shortest path (see Figure 6.10). It represents a top-down traversal of the linked structure combined with computational operations on data stored in nodes. The top level segment of the linked tree corresponds to the most significant 1 bit in the size of the array of sums. No processing for a 0 bit of the rank `k` in a linked tree is equivalent to a vertical traversal that passes through a 0 bit node. A 1 bit in the rank `k` corresponds to a traversal of a segment represented by a horizontal link in the linked tree.

Similar to the array-based algorithm implemented in the function `sum_top_down()`, this algorithm uses two addition operations on counts and pre-computed sums. The difference is that the linked representation stores in a node both a count and a sum for a partition range of a given sequence (see Figure 6.9), whereas the array representation (see Figure 6.7) stores in a cell only a sum. The counts for partition ranges are provided by the least significant 1 bits of ranks.

The `for` loop in the function `sum_top_down()` stops when the comparison operation `(count<k)` returns `false`. Therefore, all of the elements in a specified range of a partial sum have been processed. This algorithm avoids testing the remaining least significant 0 bits. For the linked representation, it means that the result is obtained before the algorithm reaches the deepest level of an index bit segment tree. Such an early exit helps us to improve the running time of the summation algorithms for both representations.

Another implementation option for the same top-down algorithm uses the following termination condition in the `for` loop:

```
for (int bit=1<<30; bit>0; bit>>=1)
```

This variant tests each bit of the rank `k` and the summation of counts represents the straightforward computation of a rank in the binary representation. In terms of the linked representation, this algorithm visits all of the levels of the structure and terminates at the node of the deepest level referred to by the given rank `k`.

6.8.2 Bottom-Up Algorithm

In addition to the top-down algorithm, the linked index bit segment tree supports the fast bottom-up summation algorithm. It can be easily seen that such an algorithm exists, since we can reverse the shortest path of the previous algorithm (see Figure 6.10).

This variant is less practical because for the best performance it requires that a user provide a pointer to a node at the deepest level. When the node is given by the user, the main remaining task of this algorithm is to find the shortest path to the first node at the top level. This is a typical search for the optimal path through all of the levels of the tree. The rank of the specified node at the deepest level and the corresponding partial sum are obtained simultaneously using pre-computed counts and sums in visited nodes. The performance of this algorithm is the same as that of the top-down algorithm.

The array representation does not place the restriction similar to providing a pointer to a node at the deepest level of a linked tree, since it can take advantage of constant-time access by the rank to any value that it stores. This is why, the implementation of the bottom-up algorithm that scans bits of the rank of a specified last element `k` is quite straightforward:

```
int sum_bottom_up(const int k)
{
    int sum = 0;
    int count = 0;
    int i = k;
    int bit = 1;

    for (bit=1; count<k; bit<<=1)
    {
        if ( k&bit )
        {
            sum += m_array[i];
            count += bit;
            i -= bit;
        }
    }

    return sum;
}
```

The code for this summation algorithm is similar to the code for the previous algorithm implemented in the function `sum_top_down()`. The main difference is that this algorithm scans the accumulated data in reverse order from the least significant bit to the most significant bit. Initially, the index into array `m_array` is equal to the input rank `i=k`. As the algorithm proceeds by testing one or more bits (moves one or more levels up in terms of the linked representation), the index decreases by the size of a processed partition range `i-=bit` (a power of 2).

6.8.3 Optimal Algorithm

The summation algorithms on arrays using counts of processed sequence elements are quite fast. Nevertheless, they are not optimal, since unnecessary tests for a 0 bit in the rank `k` increase the number of iterations and the running time. Thus, we may ask the following question: is it possible to devise a more efficient algorithm that addresses this issue? The affirmative answer to this question is the algorithm that was originally introduced by Fenwick:

```
int sum_optimal(int k)
{
        int sum = 0;

        while ( k>0 )
        {
                sum += m_array[k];
                k = k&(k-1);
        }

        return sum;
}
```

The size of the code for this algorithm is remarkably small. This fact, however, does not mean that its implementation details are trivial. In particular, it might not be obvious immediately that this algorithm is similar to the algorithm implemented in the function `sum_bottom_up()`. In terms of the linked representation, it is roughly equivalent to the bottom-up summation algorithm.

The key feature of this algorithm is the bit operation `k&(k-1)`, which removes the least significant 1 bit from the binary representation of the input rank `k`. It is a traversal operation to find and use a pre-computed value stored in the optimized array of sums. This implementation offers the following advantages.

The code does not require a special variable, such as `count`, for sequence elements that have been processed. The bit removal operation subtracts the size of a current partition range and updates the value of `k`, which represents both the index into the array and the remaining number of elements to be processed.

As an index into the implementation array `m_array[]`, the updated value of `k` provides a new position for a next iteration of this algorithm. The subtraction of the range size due to 1 bit removal moves the position towards the first value in the array of sums. Thus, the accumulated values associated with a given sequence are processed in reverse order for which the data scheme based on a reverse half-open range is the most suitable.

This algorithm does not test each bit in the input rank `k`, since the removal of the least significant 1 bit is not affected by 0 bits. The algorithm skips consecutive 0 bits and moves from a current least significant 1 bit to a next least significant 1 bit in the binary representation of the input rank `k`. For this reason, the number of iterations in this algorithm is equal to the number of 1 bits only.

Avoiding tests for 0 bits explains why this algorithm provides improved performance compared to other summation algorithms discussed above. For example, in the algorithm `sum_bottom_up()`, which tests each bit in a given rank `k` and counts processed sequence elements, the number of iterations is determined by the position of the most significant 1 bit in the input rank `k`. In the worst case, the number of iterations is equal to the total number of bits in the integer type used by the algorithm.

The fact that the running time of this array-based summation algorithm is determined by the number of 1 bits only is also interesting for the following reason. In a linked index bit segment tree, a fast summation algorithm is based on a shortest path that visits each level and contains both horizontal and vertical links. The number of vertical links in the shortest path is greater than or equal to the number of horizontal links, since a 0 bit node does not have a required link to move horizontally. Thus, the running time of such a fast summation algorithm is determined by the number of vertical rather than horizontal links. This is an important difference from the optimal array-based summation algorithm.

In terms of the shortest path, the optimal array-based algorithm provides a sequence of horizontal links only. In the linked representation, these links must be connected by vertical links. Its summation algorithm does not achieve the equivalent performance because of the fundamental limitation of the linked tree that it provides fast access only to the nearest connected neighbors of a node. An algorithm on such a tree does not have the ability to skip in constant time more than one level or several consecutive 0 bit nodes of a vertical chain.

The advantage of the array representation is that it provides constant-time access to a pre-computed value through the computation of its position. This computational method is the crucial detail to the superior performance.

The summation algorithms discussed in this section are fundamentally similar, even though specific interpretation details depend on the choice of a proper representation. For an augmented linked index bit segment tree, these algorithms are best understood in terms of the shortest path algorithms. The optimized array of pre-computed sums is less appropriate for such an interpretation because its storage is flat. The optimality of its algorithms is better expressed in terms of the minimal number of computational operations.

6.9 MODIFYING ALGORITHMS

In this section, we consider several efficient modifying algorithms on the tables of pre-computed sums. The array-based variants of these algorithms are particularly important in practical applications.

The use of ancillary data structures, such as tables of pre-computed values, not only introduces the complication of the synchronization of operations on different data structures but also can have other undesirable effects. One of them is the dramatic growth of the overall running time of a user algorithm, when corresponding operations have significant difference in the performance. To avoid this problem, the performance of modifying operations on a table of pre-computed sums must be consistent with the performance of proper operations on a given sequence. This problem dictates the choice of algorithms for the discussion.

6.9.1 Bottom-Up Construction

The algorithm for the construction of the optimized array of pre-computed sums from a given sequence is one of the simplest and fastest. The code below assumes that the implementation one-based array has been already initialized and that it stores original values of a given sequence (`m_array=array_user`). The code applies iterative processing to compute the sums associated with the partition ranges of the sequence.

```
range_size = 2;
pos_curr = 0;
dist_prev = 1;

while ( range_size<array_size )
{
    for ( pos_curr = range_size;
          pos_curr < array_size;
          pos_curr += range_size )
        m_array[pos_curr] +=
          m_array[pos_curr-dist_prev];

    dist_prev = range_size;
    range_size = range_size*2;
}
```

This algorithm mirrors the bottom-up construction algorithm for level linked data structures, such as augmented B+-trees. In terms of data initialization, the completion of one iteration of the `for` loop has the effect similar to the construction of one level in a linked data structure. A current iteration completes the computation of accumulated values for a subset of positions defined by the range size. At each position, the algorithm adds a previously computed value. The distance to this value is equal to the range size of the previous iteration. For a matching linked tree, it means that the previously computed value is stored one level below the current level. Since the range size increases by a factor of two, the number of iterations is logarithmic in the size of a given sequence. Simultaneously, the number of computational operations for each iteration drops by the same factor. Thus, the running time of this algorithm is linear in the size of a given sequence.

6.9.2 Update Value

The update operation assumes that a user provides the rank of a sequence element and the difference between the new and current values. Providing a new value is less efficient option, since it involves re-computation of a current value. In the optimized array of sums constructed for a given sequence, one element contributes to several pre-computed sums for ranges defined by the least significant 1 bits of the array indices (see Figure 6.7). The task of the supporting algorithm is to find all of the ranges that contain the given rank and save the updated values of the pre-computed sums.

```
void update_value(int k, int value_add)
{
    int size = int(m_array.size());

    while ( k<size )
    {
        m_array[k] += value_add;
        k = k + (k & -k);
    }
}
```

The information that we need to efficiently navigate the array is provided by the binary representation of the input rank. Processing starts at the position specified by the input rank and then moves the position using the sequence of bits of the rank. The key implementation details of this algorithm is the operation `k=k+(k&-k)`, which selects a next position in the array to update a pre-computed sum value. This operation represents the addition of the least significant 1 bit. In terms of the array position and the element count, it corresponds to the addition of the range size, which is a power of 2. The important feature of this operation is that it flips bits in the whole group of consecutive 1 bits and provides a new position without testing each bit in the input rank. After flipping the most significant 1 bit in the input rank, the current position is determined by one 1 bit only. Thus, the rank of a pre-computed value to be updated is asymptotically a power of 2. The example below shows the iterative effect of this operation on input integers: 16, 17 and 35.

16, 32, 64, 128, 256, 512

17, 18, 20, 24, 32, 64

35, 36, 40, 48, 64, 128

The choice of this bitwise operation allows us to reduce the total number of iterations, which depends on the array size and the number of 0 bits above the least significant 1 bit in the input rank. It makes the algorithm quite efficient, since each iteration increases the range size by at least a factor of 2 and the rank of a pre-computed value quickly exceeds the size of the implementation array. The algorithm performance is logarithmic in the worst case. For comparison, in the basic variant of a table of partial sums (sum (values[1, i]), see Figure 6.8), this operation takes linear time because it updates the accumulated value for each range [1, j] that contains the modified value: k<=j<=N.

The implementation of the update operation that we discussed is simple and requires several lines of code. It does not resize the array representation and is suitable for both dynamic and static arrays. It works without moving data stored in the cells of an array. It is optimal and highly efficient, since it modifies data in a small number of cells only. In terms of the overall performance of user algorithms, this operation addresses the issue of inefficient update operation offered by the array of pre-computed partial sums. These advantages of the update operation make the efficient array representation a popular choice for practical applications.

The implementation details of the update operation for the array representation are quite straightforward. Nevertheless, this operation is usually more challenging to understand than the fast summation algorithms. For this reason, we briefly discuss the equivalent supporting algorithm for the linked index bit segment tree, which offers a more transparent geometric interpretation.

The task of finding ranges, which contain the rank of a modified element in a given sequence, in terms of the geometric representation is equivalent to the detection of all intersections between the vertical line that passes through the position of the modified element and horizontal segments of the linked structure (see Figure 6.9). The set of intersected segments provides the ranges to update the accumulated values. For each intersected segment represented by a horizontal link, the algorithm updates the accumulated value, which is stored in the right node of the link.

The algorithm starts at the node of the deepest level that corresponds to the position of the modified value in the given sequence and moves to the top level using the shortest path. Because of the minimal set of links supported by this data structure, the algorithm visits the same nodes as the fast bottom-up summation algorithm. It means that the algorithm moves to the first vertical chain. This traversal is not consistent with the data scheme based on a reverse half-open range in which the accumulated value to be updated is stored in the right node of a horizontal link. In order to reach the required node, the algorithm should follow a horizontal link from the current node on the path to the next node at the same level. Such a link represents a segment that intersects the vertical line. The left endpoint of this segment is associated with a 0 bit node of the linked structure. A 1 bit node, which is the top node of a vertical chain, is not linked to a next node at the same level. Thus, some visited levels may not have segments that intersect the vertical line. The accumulated values at these levels remain unchanged. Passing through a 1 bit node on the shortest path without modifying accumulated data is equivalent to flipping a 1 bit in the input index while traversing values in the optimized array of pre-computed sums.

6.9.3 Append Value

In addition to the operation that updates the value of a sequence element specified by its rank, the optimized array of sums can be modified by adding new values to the end of the implementation array. Unlike the update operation that assumes that a data structure of a certain size has been already constructed, the operation that appends a new element is essentially a method of the construction of this data structure. This is why, the discussion of the latter operation can help us better understand the properties of the linked and array representations of the optimized table of pre-computed sums. It is important to note that the implementation of the append operation for the new data structures is quite different from that for the well-known complete binary tree. There is no analogy that would help us explain the append operation that we discuss in this section.

To get an idea how the append operation works, we start with the linked representation of the optimized table of sums, which is more suitable for the visualization of algorithms than the implicit array representation. We consider the simplest variant of the linked index bit segment tree that stores counts of sequence elements only (see Figure 6.5). The algorithm for the array representation can be easily obtained from the algorithm for the linked representation.

Since the new linked data structure has quite complex connectivity compared to basic data structures that support sequences, to get an idea how the append operation works, we need a model of the linked index bit segment tree that ignores less significant details. The property that enables us to reduce the complexity is that the number of horizontal links, the number of elements in a sequence and the number of vertical chains are all equal. This is essentially the property of a linked list. The difference is that a node, as a basic element of the structure, is replaced with a vertical chain of nodes.

We can use this similarity for the explanation of the append operation by viewing the linked index bit segment tree as a sequence of vertical chains of nodes connected by horizontal links. Within this model, the operation is as simple as adding to the end a new vertical chain, which is connected by a new horizontal link. In terms of the analogy with a linked list, this operation is similar to appending to the tail a node with a new data element.

The implementation of this operation on a linked list is simple because it is a one level data structure. The complexity of the same operation on the linked index bit segment tree is caused by the fact that it provides several levels to link a new vertical chain. To implement the append operation we need to know how to choose the right level to create the new horizontal link that connects the new vertical chain. Note that if we find the proper level this will automatically provide all other related data and structural elements: the count of sequence elements, the length of the new segment represented by the new horizontal link and the number of nodes in the new vertical chain.

The selection criteria that help us to develop the supporting algorithm follow from the structural invariants. Each node is an end of at most one horizontal link. We are not allowed to connect a new vertical chain to a 1 bit node, which is the right node of an existing horizontal link.

An appropriate node is not included in any horizontal link yet. This is a 0 bit node, which stores zero count. It becomes the left end node of a new horizontal link. However, a vertical chain has only one 1 bit node and normally several 0 bit nodes. In addition, there are might be different vertical chains with such nodes. The set of potentially suitable nodes is still too wide and we need yet another criterion.

To reduce the number of search options we can apply the general principle of the optimal organization of a data structure. It requires that for the best performance each new structural element should be as small as possible to keep a data structure compact. In the context of the implementation of the append operation, it implies that the new horizontal link, as a segment, must have the minimal possible length and the new vertical chain must have the minimal possible height. Now, the search problem has been reduced to finding the lowest level with the 0 bit node that meets the connectivity requirements described above.

The efficient algorithm is based on the bottom-up search for the specified 0 bit node. It starts at the last node of the deepest level and then moves up to the top level using the shortest path through the last node of each visited level. All of the nodes on the path are tested for the condition that allows linking the top node of a new vertical chain to the currently visited node. The search ends at the first 0 bit node on the path, which is not included in a horizontal link. The new vertical chain to be added has the number of nodes equal to the number of visited levels. The length of the new horizontal link is determined by the count of sequence elements 2^k at the level reached. This parameter is an invariant of the level. The length of the new link provides the horizontal position of the new chain at the deepest level. It coincides with the first position after the last node of the deepest level.

The construction of a new vertical chain is not only an important implementation detail but also has an interesting interpretation in terms of the binary representation of integers. The connectivity of the data structure requires that all of the levels below the new 1 bit node be linked. In this context, the new vertical chain prepares the data structure for future append operations by providing at several levels 0 bit nodes that can be later linked with new 1 bit nodes. The horizontal expansion of the structure caused by appending a new vertical chain is similar to that in a linked list or a dynamic array. The growth is a linear function of the size of a sequence. Less trivial is how the data structure grows in the vertical dimension, which is associated with the binary representation of integers. This growth is quite slow, since it is logarithmic in the number of sequence elements. The effect of asymmetric growth in two dimensions can be best seen in the diagram of the linked index bit segment tree when the size of a given sequence is 2^k-1.

For a specific example, consider a sequence, which contains 23 elements (see Figure 6.11). After the append operation, its new size is 23 + 1 = 24.

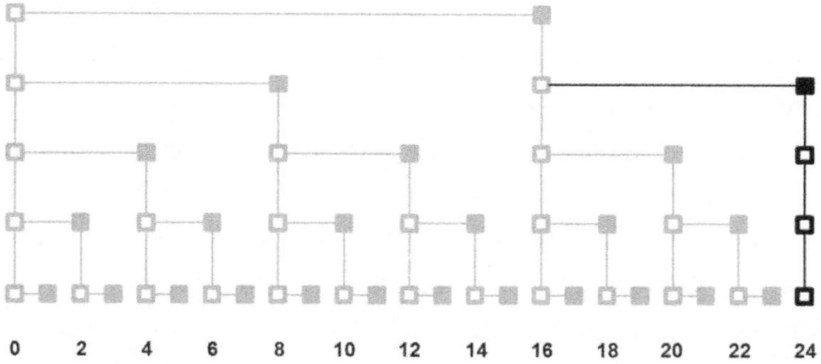

Figure 6.11: Illustration of the append operation on the linked index bit segment tree prepared for 23 data elements. The new vertical chain and horizontal link are drawn in black. 0 bit nodes are empty, 1 bit nodes are filled.

The operands of this operation have the following values of bits of the size:

1 0 1
0 0 1
1 + 0 = 0
1 0 0
1 1 0

The append operation flips all of the least significant 1 bits and the least significant 0 bit. The four least significant bits of the new size 24 shown in black correspond to the values of counts in nodes of the new vertical chain (see Figure 6.11), which connects four lowest levels of this linked index bit segment tree. In terms of comparison with operations on integers, the append operation on this data structure represents a sophisticated variant of the addition of one. The construction of a new vertical chain with a connecting horizontal link is equivalent to appending to the data structure a new count of sequence elements, which is a power of 2, in two different representations. In the count value, the length of the horizontal link is linear, whereas the height of the vertical chain is logarithmic. The vertical chain supports bits flipping identical to the increment operation on an integer in its binary representation.

The running time of this algorithm depends on the number of visited levels. Since the total number of levels in the linked index bit segment tree is logarithmic in the size of a given sequence, the algorithm has logarithmic performance in the worst case. On average, however, the algorithm does not visit all of the levels of the data structure. It normally passes through a small number of the lowest levels only. This property is potentially useful for the efficient construction of the data structure from a user sequence. In this aspect, the append operation provides a reasonable alternative to other construction methods.

Similar to the augmented B+-trees that we considered before, the linked index bit segment tree that supports fast summation algorithms is augmented with both counts of sequence values and corresponding sums. The append operation on such a data structure involves both counts and pre-computed sums. The optimized array of sums provides efficient sequence facilities that make unnecessary storing counts of sequence values. The equivalent array-based algorithms operate on pre-computed sums only. Thus, the array-based algorithm of the append operation can be implemented as the bottom-up search for the least significant 0 bit in the rank of the last value, which is combined with the summation of values in the visited cells. The following function uses a resizable array `m_array[]` implemented with the C++ standard container `std::vector<T>`.

```
void append_value(const int value_in)
{
    int sum = value_in;
    int k = int(m_array.size()) - 1;
    int bit_level = 1;

    while ( k&bit_level )
    {
        sum += m_array[k];
        k -= bit_level;

        bit_level <<= 1;
    }

    // append the accumulated value
    m_array.push_back(sum);
}
```

The algorithm starts at the position of the last value in the implementation array `m_array[]`. If the least significant bit in the rank `k` of the last value is 0, the algorithm appends the new value to the end of the implementation array and terminates. Otherwise, it enters into the `while` loop, which scans from the least significant bit to the most significant bit the sequence of bits of the binary representation of the rank `k` of the last value. This loop implements the search for the first 0 bit in `k` by testing each bit `(k&bit_level)`. If a current bit is 1 bit, an iteration adds the pre-computed value stored in the current cell to the sum of all processed values of a given sequence `sum+=m_array[k]` and moves `k` to a next position. As the index into the implementation array, `k` can be updated using two equivalent methods. The method, which counts processed elements, subtracts the size of the current partition range `k-=bit_level`. The other method removes the least significant 1 bit `k=k&(k-1)`. When the loop terminates, the accumulated value `sum` is appended to the end of the implementation array `m_array[]`.

The array-based implementation of the append operation is similar to the implementation of the bottom-up summation algorithm. Both algorithms compute the resulting value while scanning bits of a rank from the least significant bit to the most significant bit. The difference is in the termination condition that stops the scan and summation. The summation algorithm scans all of the bits up to the most significant 1 bit in a rank, whereas the append operation scans only the first least significant 1 bits.

The performance characteristics of this array-based algorithm are the same as for the linked representation. Its worst-case running time is logarithmic. It implies that the append operation is less efficient than the same operation on the array of partial sums, which takes constant time. Nevertheless, this algorithm guarantees high performance of the incremental construction of an optimized array of sums from a given sequence, since the worst-case logarithmic time of a single operation is a rare event. For each second iteration, the index for a new value is odd. The insertion of the new value at this position is a constant time operation that involves the new value only. Each fourth iteration involves two values, each eighth iteration involves four values and so on.

6.9.4 Remove Last Value

For the case when a user algorithm removes the last value from its sequence, we need the operation to update pre-computed data, which is the inverse of the append operation. The implementation of this operation is almost as simple as that for a dynamic array or a linked list, because the optimized table of the pre-computed values represents a sequence and because any value at a given position in the table does not depend on any other value in a subsequent position.

In the array representation, the operation deletes the last pre-computed value from the implementation array of partition range sums. If we use the C++ standard container `std::vector<T>` as a resizable array, then the implementation of this operation calls the member function `pop_back()`.

```
void remove_last()
{
    m_array.pop_back();
}
```

For the linked representation of the optimized table of pre-computed data, this is an operation on a sequence of vertical chains. Similar to a linked list, we remove the last vertical chain of nodes and the horizontal link that connects the chain with the remaining constituents of the linked structure.

6.10 ADDRESSING LIMITATIONS

The summation algorithms are of great importance for numerous practical applications. As the problems increase in the size, the linear performance of sequential summation becomes unsatisfactory. This performance issue can be addressed with the tables of pre-computed sums, which support highly efficient computation of the sum of values in any range of a given sequence. The optimized array-based table of sums offers efficient algorithms for the computation of a partial sum and for the update value operation, whereas the array of partial sums offers only one efficient algorithm for summation. Because of this advantage, the optimized table of sums is the preferable choice for processing of large datasets. However, it is important to remember that the table is an auxiliary data structure fine-tuned for several efficient algorithms only. As a single data structure, it has drawbacks that limit its application area.

Some limitations of the optimized table of pre-computed sums are the price that we pay for its high space efficiency. The table does not store all of the values of a given sequence. It contains only every second value at odd positions. Without the original data a missing value must be computed. The simplest method to obtain a value at an even rank is to use the difference between two partial sums: `sum(k)-sum(k-1)`, but this method is not as efficient as the subscript operator. It leads to a suboptimal performance of a user algorithm and complicates the code. For this reason, the optimized table of sums is not a good choice for an efficient representation of a mathematical sequence.

In terms of the range queries, the optimized table of sums provides adequate support for the range sum. Similar to finding a single value, it is based on the fast computation of two partial sums and the subtraction, which is the inverse of the addition. The table also enables us to efficiently compute the minimum and the maximum of the first values in a given sequence. However, there are no equivalent facilities for arbitrary range queries, because there are no inverses of these important operations. The limited support for range queries means that the efficiency and generality required for the representation of a semigroup cannot be achieved with the optimized table of sums.

One of the most important drawbacks of the optimized table of sums is associated with the insertion and deletion of values at arbitrary positions in a given sequence. Subsequent updating an array-based table is quite costly not only because of moving but also because of re-computing a large number of sum values in the table.

Maintaining a copy of the original data leads to loss of space efficiency and issues associated with the use of several data structures. The synchronization of operations on different data structures increases the implementation complexity. The differences in the performance characteristics of operations can seriously slow down the user algorithm.

The relatively small set of efficient operations and the relatively long list of limitations undeniably show that the array-based optimized table of sums is not a general purpose data structure. Its use is appropriate in simple applications. The evolution of a software product increases the likelihood of a performance bottleneck and implies that a user algorithm should be prepared to deal with this problem. The straightforward approach is to find another data structure with the most efficient operations that meet new user requirements.

Whenever possible, the primary choice is the array-based algorithms and data structures, such as a complete binary tree or a segment tree. This choice is optimal not only in terms of performance but also in terms of the cost of development and maintenance. The highly efficient array representation of a data structure takes advantage of a simple rigid structure with a fixed number of children for a parent node. The drawback of such an inflexible structure is that it does not provide efficient operations that modify datasets and causes performance degradation in applications dealing with frequent insertions and deletions. These issues of rigid structures can be best addressed with red-black trees and B+-trees, which implement re-balancing methods that preserve structural invariants.

In terms of the development of efficient general purpose algorithms, the best practical choice is a B-tree or a B+-tree. This type of trees offers attractive facilities to design and implement both basic and advanced variants. The global balance allows us to avoid the complexity of a forest of trees in processing of user datasets of arbitrary size. The flexible structure supports fine tuning the performance of algorithms using different types of node connectivity and the adjustment of the branching factor. These trees also give developers a choice of an array, linked or combined representation. The B+-trees that store each group of children in a dynamic array are normally more efficient than their equivalent linked variants.

The basic variants of B+-trees offer satisfactory facilities in terms of efficient primary algorithms for search, insertion and deletion. This variety can be extended using the method of augmenting. The most important for practical applications are the fast algorithms for counting, summation and range minimum/maximum queries. Since all of the algorithms and operations are provided by one data structure, it is effective and efficient in the general purpose representation of a mathematical set, sequence and semigroup.

For the most challenging problems and applications, B-trees and B+- trees have another important ability of integrating small size efficient data structures by storing them in nodes of a tree instead of raw data. The array-based data structures, such as considered in this chapter, have particularly attractive properties for these applications. This design method combines the strengths of different types of data structures.

Over the past several decades, electronic computing devices fully replaced mechanical computing devices, such as abacus, which were in practical use for hundreds if not thousands of years. On modern computer systems, one of the earliest types of data structures supported by programming languages was the linked list. The subsequent introduction of arrays had a dramatic effect on the applicability of the linked lists and more generally linked data structures. The significant progress in computer hardware pushes the boundary of the application area of arrays towards the larger and larger sizes of problems. The technological changes make upgrading hardware one of the practical methods to improve performance characteristics of computer systems. Programs using portable code allow for the smooth transition with the minimal amount of effort. Because of this trend, arrays are now a good choice for a wide variety of programming solutions and largely superseded linked data structures.

Nevertheless, it is unlikely that arrays will replace linked data structure to the same degree as modern computers replaced abacus. In terms of processing of large datasets, linked data structures have the important advantage over arrays. Their operations can avoid costly copying of data elements by using much cheaper operations of re-linking nodes. In particular, the running time of their split and join operations is logarithmic in the size of a dataset. The efficiency of these operations on large subsets of data is close to that of a modifying operation on a single element. By replacing arrays with such linked data structures, the running time of a user algorithm can be reduced from linear to logarithmic. This is a substantial improvement for practical applications. For this reason, the linked data structures, such as balanced trees and B+-trees, will remain valuable tools in efficient processing of constantly growing volumes of data.

The choice of the best time and space efficient data structure is never trivial in the real-life software development. There is no single data structure suitable for all of the possible types of applications. The goal of achieving high efficiency cannot, however, ignore the generality aspect when the scale of a project becomes medium or large. Finding the right level of abstraction is important for the implementation of reusable algorithms, classes of data structures and libraries. In addition, a programming solution should balance the cost of development and its quality.

6.11 SUMMARY

The effective use of array-based data structures and algorithms is important in solving practical problems. However, the implicit nature of array representations of data structures can make them challenging for understanding and analyzing algorithms. In such situations, we can take advantage of the fact that basic principles of the design of algorithms are not highly sensitive to implementation details and devise a matching linked representation of a data structure. The linked representation allows us to better visualize the search path or the computational path of an algorithm.

The array representation of a segment tree with the structure of a perfect binary tree is one of the most space efficient and one of the simplest to implement. It offers a number of fast algorithms for important applications. The disadvantages of this tree are associated with its rigid structure and a fixed size.

A data scheme determines the space efficiency of a data structure and performance characteristics of algorithms that it supports. The fact that one structure can be used with different data schemes provides great opportunity for designing efficient algorithms.

After the removal of each second horizontal child link from a segment tree, the resulting segment tree provides a smaller variety of efficient primary algorithms. In particular, it is less efficient in the representation of a sequence than its predecessor. The new tree is no longer a level linked tree, but it has the connectivity of a binary tree that can support complicated data structures. The new connectivity facilitates the efficient algorithms for the computation of a partial sum and for the update value operation. It also removes the restriction of a segment tree on the size of a sequence.

The array-based variant of the new segment tree represents an optimized table of pre-computed sums. In large scale applications, such an optimized array of sums outperforms an array of partial sums because it offers not only the fast partial sum algorithm but also the fast algorithm to update a value. Its high space and time efficiency is due to the partitioning method using the binary representation of indices into a sequence. At the same time, the optimized table of sums is not a general purpose data structure, since it has a number of limitations.

The choice of the optimal data structure is never trivial in practical applications dealing with constantly growing volumes of data. The advanced programming solutions combine the strengths of both array and linked data structures.

Annotated Bibliography

- T.H. Cormen, C.E. Leiserson, R.L. Rivest and C. Stein. *Introduction to Algorithms.* Second Edition, MIT Press and McGraw-Hill, Cambridge (MA), 2001.
- R. Sedgewick and K. Wayne. *Algorithms.* Fourth Edition, Addison-Wesley, Boston, 2011.

These classical books cover a wide variety of algorithms and data structures. They also include introduction to the method of augmenting data structures.

- B. Stroustrup. *The C++ Programming Language.* Third Edition, Addison Wesley, 2007.

Beyond the complete description of the C++ programming language and its standard library, this book provides valuable guidelines for using programming techniques to find the right level of abstraction in the real-world software development.

About the Author

Vadim Stadnik received his Ph.D. degree in physics and mathematics from Moscow State University. He has many years of experience in fundamental scientific and applied research. He has been involved in the development of innovative software products and performance optimization of programming solutions for large scale problems. His research and technical interests include computational mathematics, artificial intelligence and scientific programming.

Feedback

I would really appreciate your feedback to improve the contents of this book. You can also post a review on Amazon that would help potential readers to make the decision whether to read this book.

Thank you for reading this book and for your support!

Made in the USA
Monee, IL
04 November 2026

67378680R00125